THE
Great British
COUNTRYSIDE

THE
Great British
COUNTRYSIDE

A LIVING HISTORY

CHRISTOPHER SOMERVILLE

David & Charles

For Andrew, my first companion in the countryside

Photographic Acknowledgements
Britain on View: pages 11, 14, 15, 18, 22, 23, 30, 37, 41, 46,
51, 55, 62, 71, 75, 82, 86, 87, 95, 99, 103, 111, 115, 122, 123,
134, 143, 147, 151, 155, 163, 167, 170, 174.
Derby City Museum: page 12.
Salisbury and South Wiltshire Museum: page 19.
Syndication International Ltd: pages 20, 31, 127, 162.
Ryedale Folk Museum: page 30
Peter Wakely: pages 59, 83, 90.
Coate: pages 91, 150, 151.
Roger Rogers: pages 94, 146, 147.
Chiltern Open Air Museum: page 139.
Sacrewell: page 142.
Nature Conservancy Council: pages 155, 170.

British Library cataloguing in Publication Data
Somerville, Christopher
  The Great British countryside.
  I. Title
  508.41

ISBN 0-7153-9832-6

Designed by Michael Head

Typeset by Ace Filmsetting Ltd, Frome, Somerset,
and printed in Hong Kong by Imago Publishing Ltd
for David & Charles plc
Brunel House, Newton Abbot, Devon

CONTENTS

ACKNOWLEDGEMENTS

I would especially like to thank John and Rosemary Berry of Billingsmoor, Devon; Bob Peters of Plashett Park, Sussex; Paul Dunsby of Cotswold Orchards, Worcestershire; James Stamper of West Farm, Suffolk; Julian Proctor of Onslow Farm, Lincolnshire; Bill Richardson of High Shaw, Northumberland; Tony and Irene Mouat of Clingera, Island of Uist, Shetland; Jerry Harding of Pentood Uchaf, Dyfed; and Kevin McAuley of Broughshane, Co Antrim, for their kindness in showing me around their farms and taking time and trouble to answer my questions. Thanks are also due to the following officials of the National Farmers' Union for recommending such approachable and exemplary farmers: Anthony Gibson of South West Region office, Gareth Evans of East Sussex County Branch, B. Johnson of Evesham office, Mike Marshall-Hollingsworth of East Anglia Region office, K. Parnell of Holland (Lincolnshire) Branch and Beverley Scott of Northumberland Branch. I am grateful to Sam McEwen of the Department of Agriculture of Northern Ireland and to the Bristol office of the Soil Association for their help.

I would also like to thank Elaine Viner, Bill Richards, Faith Glasgow, Alison Elks and Penny Grigg for all their hard work; and my parents, for my childhood in the Gloucestershire countryside.

INTRODUCTION

The Gloucestershire village where I grew up lay along a winding road that led nowhere. It looped away from the rush and roar of the main highway, circled among widely spaced houses and old apple orchards for a mile or so and then straggled back to meet the outside world again. In summer cow parsley, nettles and dog roses grew unchecked in the hedges. At 6 years old I was too small to see over their thick green screen. The road and its forward view – a cider apple tree hanging over the next corner, a gateway into a cornfield – were the limits of my world whenever I wandered from home.

At the bottom of the village the duck pond lay on a bend of the road and here the Green Lane ran off at right angles, a low road to adventure, familiar from countless expeditions with my friend Andrew, but always rich with the promise of new delights. It was a muddy old track at all times of the year, a boggy slog between abandoned orchards, whose sucking mud could be relied on to pluck off first one gumboot and then the other, leaving us to squelch in sodden socks to the drier ruts at the side. In winter the ruts were skinned over with milky panes of ice and the drainage ditch became a sliding rink that creaked ominously as we inched out on to its fracturing surface.

The Green Lane ended at an ancient cattle trap, a box of stout timbers where the village's farmers in times gone by had corralled their herds from the Big Meadow that lay beyond. This was the prize at the end of the quest: an enormous field that stretched away to a line of bushes marking the course of a disused coal canal on the edge of sight. On the Big Meadow we ran like unleashed puppies for hours at a stretch, persecuted water rats in the canal with sticks, stones and airgun pellets, slid and crashed on the ice of January and launched hopeless home-made boats on the floods of February. To us it was a giant playground, each one of its pollarded willows and marshy hollows intimately known, but always offering more secrets, more things to do, more space to explore.

This was my childhood countryside – a couple of low-lying square miles in the Severn Valley, hardly a blob on the Ordnance Survey map that lies before me as I write. One day Andrew and I ventured further afield and, like Mole in *The Wind in the Willows*, found ourselves on the banks of a great river – the Severn, flowing in a majestic curve under Wainlode Hill on its way from Tewkesbury to Gloucester. Gradually I extended my range, wandering in the fields on the other side of the main road, walking the 5 miles (8km) into Tewkesbury along lanes and through fields that were alien territory. But Green Lane and Big Meadow were the bedrock on which all my notions of countryside were founded. Elsewhere there were tall hills, seashores, moors, mountains; but they were as remote as the deserts of Africa or the jungles of Brazil.

Returning to the village as an adult, it came as a shock to see just how small was the compass of all those childhood expeditions. Now I was aware of the range of hills that stood out beyond the Big Meadow, the church towers of neighbouring villages poking up all round the horizon, the scores of other lanes and footpaths that linked into my own little network. But then, at 6 and 7 and 8 years old, they were not only unexplored: they were unseen, undreamed of.

Today, in the knowledge of all the tremendous variety of countryside from end to end of the British Isles, those few flat acres of Gloucestershire still tug at the heart strings. They have been in my mind all through the writing of this book. The British countryside, in all its beauty and its rich history of constant change, is our greatest national treasure. It could so easily be nibbled away, polluted and destroyed, its heritage forgotten and its future blighted by thoughtless development and over-exploitation, by a lack of care and vigilance. The work of the countryside centres, the open-air museums and national parks featured in this book is invaluable. I hope that you will be inspired to visit and enjoy them – perhaps to join in their great range of activities – and also to roam the countryside with the Ramblers' Association, to learn about its bird life with the Royal Society for the Protection of Birds, to explore its clifftops and woodlands with the National Trust, to roll up your sleeves and dig for its eventual victory over decline and abuse with the British Trust for Conservation Volunteers.

These are practical ways in which ordinary people can play a part in the nurture of our countryside and safeguard it for future generations of children setting out to delight in their own Green Lanes and their own Big Meadows.

CHAPTER 1
THE SHAPE OF THINGS

Under the green and pleasant skin of Britain lies a twisted skeleton of rock bones. The most ancient are nearly 3,000 million years old, some of the oldest rocks in the world. The newest are still being formed, infinitely slowly. In the south and east of Britain the bones lie in smoothly flowing shapes, while in the north and west they rear up, bent, contorted, turned upside down and back to front, poking rude fingers through the skin of green. To look at the hanging curtains of volcanic lava that form the Antrim coast in Northern Ireland and the Scottish isles, or the snake-like curves of the limestone strata at Lulworth Cove in Dorset, is to see vigorous movement caught and held in suspension. The geological map of Britain shows the frozen animation of these underlying rocks – a sinuous flow of movement towards the south-eastern corner of the country, from the stony harshness of the Scottish and Welsh mountains across to the successive layers of limestone, chalk and clay that push ever softer and more fertile frontiers down into East Anglia, Surrey and Kent. It is high, hard and old in the top left-hand corner of the picture; low, soft and new in the bottom right.

This flattening, smoothing and softening south-easterly flow influences every last detail of the way the British countryside looks today. It determines why there are no rolling chalk downs in Scotland or Northern Ireland, and no jagged slate mountains in Bedfordshire. It puts the granite sparkle in the field walls of Cornwall and the creamy richness in those of the Cotswolds. It fills the silos of the grain barons in Norfolk and the hoppers of British Coal in south Yorkshire. Without this wonderful variety under the surface of Britain we would have no dales, no downs, no moors; no cwms, no glens, no fens: that diversity of landscape in a small area that overseas visitors envy and the British generally take for granted.

The age of the oldest rocks in the north-west of Britain can only be guessed at. The origin of the earth – whether it was caused by a big bang, a spin-off from the sun or an act of God – has been put at 4,500ma (million years ago). The magma, or molten rock core, probably began to develop a hard outer crust in the Scottish Highlands and islands some 2,500ma, forming igneous rocks with their angular names: granite, dolerite, gabbro, basalt. Some rocks were baked, boiled and squeezed so mightily that their very internal structures and chemical make-up were changed: gneiss, schist, quartzite – the metamorphic rocks. These primitive lumps of dull or sparkling material were gradually ground down by rain, wind and earthquakes over a period of hundreds of millions of years into powder, forming sea-bed sheets of sedimentary rock that were many miles

Geological Museum of North Wales, Bwlchgwyn, Wrexham, Clwyd, North Wales. Geological displays featuring relief models, maps, photographs and thousands of specimens. Also display of industrial relics, a rock garden where you can collect specimens and a geological trail through an old silica quarry.

Giant's Causeway and Antrim Coast, Bushmills, Co Antrim. World Heritage Site and National Nature Reserve. Basalt and other volcanic rock formations; wreck site of Spanish Armada treasure ship *Girona* at Port-na-Spaniagh; visitor centre.

Brimham Rocks Information Centre, Brimham House, Summerbridge, Harrogate, North Yorkshire. Exhibition and tape/slide programme on geology and history of Brimham Rocks – millstone grit stacks on nearby Brimham Moor. Information Centre is in the old shooting lodge.

Bare volcanic majesty of the ancient rocks of Snowdon.

thick. Later, subterranean upheavals and eruptions hoisted them clear of the water again, and twisted, bent and buckled them into jagged mountains that were as yet unclothed by any vegetation. All this activity took place over perhaps 2,000 million years, laying down the basis for the Scottish Highlands and islands, the eastern hills of Northern Ireland and the basalt columns of the Giant's Causeway on the Antrim coast, the highest peaks of the Lake District and North Wales and the granite heart of Dartmoor and Cornwall.

From about 600ma, the details of the formation of rock types become clearer, although the south-easterly flow does not settle into regular cross-country bands of successive age until it reaches the S-shaped belts of reddish sandstone, marl and clay that were laid down between 250ma and 225ma from North Yorkshire across the central Midlands, spreading south west to southern Devon.

North and west of those belts are the hills of central Northern Ireland, central Scotland, the Scottish Borders and the Welsh mountains, a splendid tumbled confusion of grit, slates, schists, shale, sandstone and older rocks that were ground up small and squeezed together under gigantic pressures from colliding continental plates. Some of these ancient mountain ranges formed 300 or 400 million years ago probably rose as high as 16,000ft (5,000m), but they have been worn away since then into stumps less than a fifth of their original height. Such is the power of wind and weather, which have shaped our countryside since earliest times and which continue to do the same slow work today.

On the upper and older side of those central belts are the old red sandstone of North Devon and Cornwall, the limestone and gritstone uplands of the Pennines, and the coalfields of the North East and of central Lancashire and Yorkshire, Nottinghamshire and South Wales. Some 400ma a great desert filled the centre of England and parts of Scotland; its sands were blown or washed together to form the old red sandstone. The Pennine limestone was formed about 50 million years later of innumerable shells and other remains of deep-water marine creatures; the gritstone was formed of sand and stone particles that were brought down by prehistoric rivers to their estuaries. Both limestone and gritstone rose clear of the seas in one era of upheavals, sank in the next era with their covering of vegetation and rose again after millions more years with that vegetation now squashed and compressed into coal. A speeded-up film of the movements of Britain's landscape over the eras would show at first a grey and black mass shot through with fiery red, writhing and jerking like clay in the hands of a mad invisible potter. Then a green blanket is thrown over the mass, beneath which it continues to swell and contract like Boy Scouts fighting in a tent. Every now and then it is plunged into a bath of water to continue its activities below the surface, bursting out again once more naked before slipping beneath another green blanket and more water – a display of dynamic energy and force.

Wildlife of the Carboniferous Period.

BEAUTIFUL OOLITE

East of the central belts, the younger and softer rocks fan downwards into the fertile lowlands of eastern England. A band of superbly beautiful and readily worked building stone runs from Devon and Dorset through Somerset (where it forms the characteristic deep golden 'hamstone') to Bath and the Cotswolds (the famous creamy-yellow stone of the field walls and medieval barns, houses and churches); north-east from there through Oxfordshire and the eastern Midlands, and continuing north as the spine of the Lincolnshire Wolds as far as the Humber. A final outburst appears around the coasts of the North Yorkshire moors. This is oolitic limestone – tiny grains of sand enveloped by deposits of calcium carbonate, full of lime and shell remains – which was formed on the bed of clear tropical seas some 200ma. In the clever hands of man this thin band of light stone has been made to beautify and enrich the 300-mile strip of countryside it crosses.

CHALK

Younger clays and greensand lie next to the oolite, and their eastern neighbour is the underlying material of much of southern England – chalk. The Great Chalk Sea that covered much of Europe 100 million years ago was alive with tiny creatures known to today's geologists as *Foraminifera* – minute single-celled beings with shells that were rich in calcium. As they died, their shells settled on to the sea bed and built up as chalk in layer upon layer at a rate of about 3ft (1m) every 100,000 years. They must have been accumulating for almost 50 million years, for the highest point of the chalk, Walbury Hill in Hampshire, reaches 1,000ft (300m) in height and the chalk goes down a further 650ft (200m) below the sea – a vivid practical illustration of such mind-boggling numbers.

Most of Britain was covered 100 million years ago with a gently curving and smoothly undulating white chalk blanket. But some 70ma, as the dinosaurs were beginning to die out, came another period of great convulsive eruptions, earth crust movements and continental plate collisions. The hard and ancient volcanic rocks in the North and West broke through their chalk covering, and rain and wind eroded away almost all of what remained. In the South and East the chalk moved violently in rhythm with the harder rocks underneath – the greensands and sandstones. On the Weald of Kent it bulged up into a great dome whose high and exposed summit weathered away down to the underlying sand and clay. Left clinging to the edges of the dome were the chalk ridges we know now as the North and South Downs. In the Isle of Wight the chalk was shoved through 90° and made to stand on end. In Purbeck on the Dorset coast it was squeezed and buckled into crazy curves. But on the Wiltshire and Hampshire downs, where it was rippled into gently rolling waves, the chalk covering survived virtually intact.

After these subterranean excitements, the British landscape settled down into its familiar shape, the hard and high old rocks of the west sloping to the softer lowlands of the east and south. There was still some shaping to be done, however, in the depositing of mighty beds of pebbles, clay and sand by the three giant rivers that flowed to the East Anglian coast, along the Thames Valley and through the Hampshire basin inland of what is now the Solent.

ICE AGES

Between about 600,000BC and 12,000BC there was a succession of four great Ice Ages, during which the ice sheets put the finishing touches to the rough-hewn handiwork of volcanic eruption, earth movement, sea inundation, river sculpture, frost, wind and rain. The high mountains of Northern Ireland, Scotland and Wales were gouged into trough-like valleys by massive sheets of moving ice up to a mile (1.6km) thick. Their outlines were sharpened by frost which shattered and splintered any projections. Lower rock in Scotland and Wales, along with the North of England, the Pennines and parts of the East Midlands, was smoothed and rounded if it was soft and cut into jagged peaks if it was hard. Further to the south-east, the valley bottoms became choked with the debris of rubble and boulders that were carried by the ice sheets. In the warmer periods between the Ice Ages the thaws of spring released thundering masses of water that scoured out bowl-shaped valleys in the chalk downs and brought more silt, gravel and rubble down to the eastern coasts and flat lands – alien items such as quartzite, basalt and granite which the glaciers had picked up further north and left behind as they retreated. All this Ice Age rubbish, as it settled and began to break down, lent a variety and richness to the alluvial soils of these eastern and southern river basins and coast lands that today helps to give them the agricultural advantage they enjoy over the rest of the country. But the human population of Britain just after the last Ice Age had not yet learned that the soil was something from which men could wrest the means of sustaining life.

STONE AGE MAN

There had been a human presence in Britain at the end of the first Ice Age in about 250,000BC, and periods of occupation between the following Ice Ages as the climate warmed up and returning vegetation was followed by returning animals. Knowledge of these extremely primitive people is almost completely obscured by the great number of millennia that separates modern man from them, but at least two things about them are certain: they must have been hunters and they must have been present in tiny numbers. Much more is known about the Paleolithic or Early Stone Age nomads who arrived some time after 12,000BC by way of the land bridge that then joined the southern coast of Britain to the northern coast of France. They found an adequate food supply among the herds of mammoth, aurochs, elk, woolly rhinoceros and reindeer grazing on the tundra vegetation – lichens, mosses, sedges, a few varieties of grass, some sub-arctic plants – that had crept in to replace the ice.

Durdle Door, Dorset: soft chalk being eaten away by the sea.

The Seven Sisters cliffs in East Sussex – ramparts of solid chalk.

The Paleolithic nomads spent their days hunting and gathering what edible roots and berries they could find, and their nights in trying to keep warm and safe by a fire. Their effect on the landscape was minimal. Man the great changer, some of whose modern activities threaten the very existence of the countryside, was then entirely insignificant in the harsh post-Ice Age environment. But his impact was soon to be felt.

Slowly the climate warmed and the winds lost their deadly chill. Wide grasslands developed and trees began to get a root-hold – alder and hazel at first in the wet thawed ground; later, the cold-resistant pines and birches. As the climate warmed around 7,500BC, a thick, broadleaved forest of oak, lime and elm spread over the landscape. The cumbersome, hairy Ice Age beasts died out and others took their place – boar and wolf, bear and red deer. The skeletons and enormous hollow antlers of the giant deer that roamed Ireland at this time are still being dug out of the bogs.

Smoothly undulating chalk downs at Cherhill, Wiltshire.

The Mesolithic (Middle Stone Age) people, who were active between about 8,000BC and 4,000BC, were clever workers of flint and wood, leather and bone. They hunted the animals of the wildwood forest as their predecessors had done, but they gradually developed a new way of working. With their stone axes they cleared sections of the forest to encourage the growth of grassland and grazing plants – shoots and leaves of rowan, birch and hazel – which they realised would attract animals and fix them to one predictable spot. There they could be judiciously culled without being scared away or hunted to local extinction. Those who can be sure of a regular meal can afford to live in settlements, even if they are only seasonal ones. So the first clearings and the first semi-permanent dwellings began to appear, along with the first stirrings of skills in animal husbandry and management of the countryside. Tribal 'ownership' of patches of land was already established by the time the pioneer farmers of the Late Stone Age made their appearance.

Neolithic (Late Stone Age) people brought fully developed farming skills with them when they crossed to Britain from the Mediterranean around 3,700BC. They came in boats, for the land bridge across the English Channel had been swamped by rising seas about three thousand years earlier. The Neolithic farmers had wheat and barley in their boats, as well as domesticated sheep and cattle. They carved their way deeper into the forest on the 'slash and burn' principle – cutting down and burning trees, but leaving the stumps in the ground to save labour. Fertilised by the ash of the burned trees, the ground would yield a reasonable crop for eight or ten years. Then the farmer slashed and burned his way into the next block of forest. In an enormous area of forested land with a tiny population of fewer than twenty thousand, this worked well enough. But in upland, poorly drained areas the abandoned clearings tended not to regenerate. Instead they became waterlogged and the natural nutrients in the soil were washed away in rains or floods. In time the soil became acid and sterile, developing into blanket peat bog where nothing would grow. Many of Britain's upland peat moors and bogs, such as those in the Irish hills, on the Pennines and on Dartmoor, had already been created by Stone Age farming practices when a new wave of immigrants came to Britain in about 2,000BC, bringing with them the epoch-making secret of bronze.

THE BRONZE AGE

The Beaker Folk, who were so called because of the finely worked pottery vessels that were found in their burial sites, arrived in Britain over a period of several hundred years. They ruled southern Britain, their cleverness in the making and working of bronze giving them a decisive advantage over people who were still relying on stone implements. In their previous homelands on the Rhine they had learned how to combine copper and tin to produce a metal that was easier to work but harder and sharper than either of its constituents. Now there could be efficient cutting edges for faster

The ARC Archaeological Resource Centre, St Saviourgate, York. ARC is based in a restored medieval church. Hands-on experience of piecing together genuine archaeological finds, using techniques ranging from traditional glue-jigsaw to computer technology. Find out for yourself in the company of working archaeologists.

work with axe, knife and sword. Inroads into the forest increased. Later immigrants brought light ploughs with them, drawn by oxen, to supersede the breakable and labour-intensive digging stick.

Around the time of the arrival of the first Beaker Folk the upland area of Dartmoor was colonised, cleared of its remaining trees, used for a few hundred years and then abandoned as worked-out, sterile blanket bog. Traces of a Bronze Age landscape can still be clearly seen on the moor, especially from the air when dry conditions give special prominence to the marks on the ground. Here are the foundations of round huts, some in little clusters and some solitary; the lines of walls that once enclosed grazing areas, fields and animal pens; other walls that ran for miles and formed a grid pattern that probably marked off tracts of the moor into separate ownership. The bronze-makers found the tin they needed in the granite rocks of Dartmoor and further west in Cornwall, while the copper came from mines as far afield as Wales, Scotland and Ireland.

Death, burial and religious ritual played a big part in the lives of Bronze Age people, who were completely at the mercy of nature. They had to try to create a sense of order in such haphazard circumstances. They buried their dead in individual graves, crouched in foetal positions in round barrows, or cremated in square box-like stone chambers known as kistvaens. They erected standing stones and took on such enormous labours as the building of Stonehenge and the Avebury stone circles. Their monuments are still prominent in the landscape and their bodily remains have been investigated to the limit of modern man's scientific ability. Yet there is no way of making the roughest of guesses at their internal life, their thoughts and dreams.

THE IRON AGE

By about 600BC the Bronze Age landscape, which consisted of scattered dwellings, pastures, small corn fields, animal enclosures, burial mounds and stone circles, was dotted about all over Britain, but still it made no more than a few bare patches in the thick green covering of wildwood. Another technological revolution was about to affect the British countryside, however, introduced by the Celtic incomers from France who were skilled in the smelting and working of iron. The new material overthrew the dominance of bronze as completely as bronze had rendered obsolete the stone axe and scraper. The manufacture of bronze implements did not cease overnight; nor did the use of stone tools come abruptly to an end. Probably some people continued with the old neolithic ways all through the Bronze Age and bronze users may well have resisted the harder material for a time. But the new ploughs of the Celts, which were tipped with hard iron, opened up corn-growing for the first time, rather than sheep and cattle husbandry, as a main way of subsistence living. Iron Age farmers no longer needed to slash, burn and move on; they could plough, sow and reap their small rec-

Cambridge University Museum of Archaeology and Anthropology, Downing Street, Cambridge. Comprehensive displays of Stone, Bronze and Iron Age tools, weapons, ornaments and pottery; also Roman, Saxon and Viking.

The Wayside Museum, Zennor, Cornwall. Housed in the village's old mill. Many tools and mementoes of Cornwall's tin-mining heritage; mine trucks and trams. Also large collection of artefacts from traditional Cornish life.

Salisbury and South Wiltshire Museum, The King's House, 65 The Close, Salisbury, Wiltshire. Housed in the Salisbury residence of the abbots of Sherborne. Gallery showing how, when and by whom Stonehenge was built; tools, weapons and other finds from the site; collection of pictures of Stonehenge through the ages. Also large collection of material from earliest man to medieval times, Salisbury collections and costumes.

Alexander Keiller Museum, Avebury, Wiltshire. Archaeological finds from excavations in this area (one of the richest in Britain), including pottery, tools and animal skeletons, and a five thousand-year-old skeleton of a child. Display makes a potentially dry subject come alive.

Dorset County Museum, High West Street, Dorchester, Dorset. Many Iron Age artefacts and displays from sites all over the county. Also galleries featuring geology, natural history, archaeology, Thomas Hardy and other 'Dorset worthies', and traditional Dorset life.

West Kennet Long Barrow,
Wiltshire, built in about 2,500BC.

The settlement site at Jarlshof,
Shetland, contains remains from
Stone Age, Bronze Age, Iron Age,
Viking and medieval settlements.

Early Bronze Age objects from Salisbury Plain.

One of the Beaker Folk buried with due ceremony.

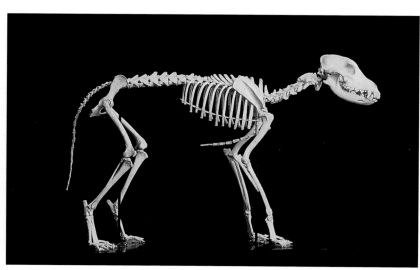

Dog of Beaker period, found buried with his master.

Stonehenge – why *did* primitive man labour to build it?

tangular fields on the tops of the downs or on hillside terraces, and live in settled villages from one generation to the next. In areas of durable building materials, such as the granite fastnesses of Cornwall, village houses could even be built in stone. A farmer could look forward to a time when his sons and grandsons might occupy his house in their turns, harvesting the fields that he had cut from the forest, rearing their pigs and sheep in the pens he had built. The idea of permanence entered men's thinking, and with it the notion of property – and especially land – was passed on and jealously guarded. Weapons that were tipped and bladed with iron were effective deterrents against attack and theft by other tribes.

As the wildwood began to fall at a greater rate than before to the iron-bladed axes, earthen ramparts were thrown up on more than two thousand hilltops across Britain to create strongholds – part fortified villages, part reinforced cattle enclosures – overlooking miles of country. 🌿 Down in the waterlogged peat moors of the Somerset Levels the dwellers sank thousands of tree trunks to form artificial islands that were connected to drier ground by wooden causeways with drawbridges. Here their wattle-and-daub huts were safe from attack. 🌿 Celts were imaginative people who were sensitive to danger from their own kind as well as from the hidden world of faeries, demons and mystical spirits with which they believed their trees, hills and rivers were filled. In Ireland they developed a rich heritage of semi-mythical history in song and story. 🌿

Woodspring Museum, Burlington Street, Weston-super-Mare, Avon.
Archaeology gallery depicting life and death in nearby Iron Age fort of Worlebury.

The Willows Peat Moors Visitor Centre, Shapwick Road, Westhay, near Glastonbury, Somerset.
Exhibition and reconstruction of the Sweet Track, wooden trackway six thousand years old that runs nearby.

About a hundred years before the birth of Christ, refugees arrived in Britain from France, in flight from the all-conquering Romans. Incoming settlers had always brought with them some revolutionary new skill, and these Belgae had the idea of attaching wheels to the plough. With the help of the wheels the oxen could drag a much heavier plough, which bit many inches deeper than the older model. Low-lying clay lands, which were stiff but fertile, could now be brought into production. The deep ploughing ripped up tree roots, too, helping the farmers in their eternal battle against the re-encroachment of the wildwood. With the opening up of these new valley farmlands, many of the old downland fields were abandoned and reverted to rough grassland. There were crops in the valleys and sheep on the downs, products of the farming system that came in at this time and came to stay.

THE ROMAN OCCUPATION

In their occupation of Britain during the first four centuries AD, the Romans changed much of the appearance of the landscape. They built great wide roads that ran in straight lines for hundreds of miles across the country. The network of by-roads that wriggled outwards from these main arteries opened up hitherto inaccessible countryside and took the plough into areas of heavy clay in which no previous road-builders had been able to make any progress. The province of Britain became one of the chief grain-baskets of the hungry Roman empire and one of its most prolific wool producers. Any land that could be brought into cultivation was attacked. Large areas of the sea-invaded fens of eastern England and of Romney Marsh – perhaps of the Somerset Levels as well – were drained with dykes and criss-crossed with causeways. Some regions that remained too wet and salt-laden for growing crops were reclaimed for cattle grazing.

Most Roman farming took place on estates whose hub was the villa, a fine house that was usually set in a sunny, south-facing and sheltered position. An estate might be as large as 100 acres (40ha) and comprised the best land in the district, especially the rich alluvial soils of the river valleys. The native Celts, who were pushed up on to the poorer, higher land, struggled to cultivate its unfruitful soil, while the Roman usurpers prospered in the fat lands below. In this way, by reclaiming the poorest and improving the best of the land, the Romans settled some sizable areas of Britain – the Fens, the Thames Valley near London, the valley of the Trent and parts of the wolds of Yorkshire. Around Gloucester they were widely established, as in a string of towns through the central Midlands to Chester. The Belgae had built a few towns – Colchester, St Albans, Winchester; but the Romans created many others – Exeter, Gloucester, London, Bath, Chester, York. They made far greater use than any previous settlers of the mineral wealth of Britain, too, as they mined lead and coal on Mendip, tin in Cornwall, silver in Derbyshire, gold in Wales, and iron and coal in the Forest of

Ulster Museum, Botanic Gardens, Belfast. Archaeological displays including Mesolithic flint artefacts, bronze and gold Bronze Age items, Iron Age Celtic metalwork, skeleton of giant Irish deer. Also geological section featuring gemstones, minerals and display on geological formation of Ireland; botany and zoology featuring all recorded species of Irish mammals and freshwater fishes, insects, molluscs, flowering plants. 'Living Sea' exhibition. Treasures from the Armada shipwreck *Gironia* are of world importance.

Yorkshire Museum, Museum Gardens, York. Roman statues, wall paintings, mosaics, tombstones, jewellery; reconstruction of a Roman kitchen; coins, tools, cutlery, etc. Also displays of Anglo-Saxon, Viking and medieval life.

Trethevy Quoit, Cornwall:
prehistoric man's burial chamber.

Silbury Hill, Wiltshire, built around
2,000BC for some great but
unguessable purpose.

Iron Age House

Chiltern Open Air Museum
Chalfont St. Giles

An Iron Age family outside their house.

Old Sarum, Wiltshire, a great late Iron Age hill fort.

Clayton Memorial Museum, Chesters Roman Fort, Walwick, near Hexham, Northumberland. Superb collection of Roman inscriptions, statues of gods and goddesses, weapons, tools, pottery, ornaments – many beautifully carved and decorated.

Dean. They quarried stone in the Isle of Purbeck and cut timber from the Wealden forest to make charcoal for iron-smelting.

Yet notwithstanding all this activity, and disregarding the military garrisons that had to be victualled and supplied, the overall effect of the Roman occupation on the landscape was not as dramatic as might be believed. The population of Britain rose to perhaps ¾ million, of which about ¼ million lived in the towns. Away from these crowded centres, the remaining inhabitants were scattered thinly across Britain's 50 million acres (20 million ha) – fewer than a million of which were under cultivation – at the rate of 100 acres (40ha) per person. In their hamlets and single farms above the productive lands of the Roman estates, sweating out a living from their ungenerous hillsides, it is doubtful whether the Celtic farmers were much bothered by the Romans and all their works. The great Roman roads themselves, purposeful as they were, made only the thinnest of thin lines in the forests as they arrowed through. Over the vast majority of the countryside no human voice had yet been heard. And for all their self-confidence and their brilliance as organisers and prime movers, the sophistication of their architecture and civil engineering, the solidity of their laws and culture, the influence of the Romans began to wane as soon as the last of them left Britain around AD406 in a last-ditch attempt to shore up their tottering empire.

Like over-protected children whose nanny has walked out, the Romano-British natives simply couldn't keep things together. The fen dykes collapsed and the fenlands reverted to marsh. The magnificent roads split apart and became mud tracks once more. The splendid villas crumbled into their weed-choked fields. The wildwood began to recapture its lost territory. When Anglo-Saxon invaders ventured along those ruined highways into the heart of southern Britain half a century after the Romans had left, it was as if the long civilisation had never been.

ANGLO-SAXONS

One tends to think of the six centuries between the Roman withdrawal and the Norman Conquest as a welter of darkness and bloody deeds, the Dark Ages in truth, during which the whole country was smothered under one gigantic forest heaving with dangerous wild animals and marauding Norsemen. But in fact the Anglo-Saxons, after a certain amount of fire and sword, settled down to a reasonably steady arrangement of adjoining kingdoms – the four most influential were Wessex, Mercia (the Midlands), East Anglia and Northumberland. The new invaders came across from the Low Countries in waves of settlement from the fifth to the seventh century, establishing themselves in villages which were often only a mile or two apart. The houses of these villages were often grouped around a central green or scattered about as circumstances dictated, but the majority of the settlements were linear affairs along the rivers that people relied on for irrigation, drinking, washing, transport and protection. Like the Romans, the more powerful of the Anglo-Saxon leaders had large estates, which were separated by earthen boundary banks. In troubled times they refortified some of the old and long-abandoned Iron Age hill camps and built new defensive earthworks against attackers. As the population increased, so did the necessity for an effective system of law. However, what evolved was not a military-style legal system imposed by a hierarchy, but codes of behaviour and punishment that were worked out at meetings and councils.

The demands of agriculture in uncertain times brought people to rely on and help one another far more than in the past. Ox teams were co-operatively owned, as were many of the ploughs. A poor man would work for more powerful neighbours in return for their protection or help in hard times. He could hope eventually to buy his own ox and join a team, which in turn gave him the right to a piece of land. In this way were germinated the seeds of the feudal system which dominated everyday life in medieval Britain.

The teams of oxen that pulled the Anglo-Saxons' heavy ploughs numbered up to eight. These long, cumbersome teams could not be turned easily once they were under way. The Anglo-Saxon field, therefore, in contrast to the smallish, squarish Celtic version, elongated over as much as a 'furrow-long' or furlong, in which the lumbering oxen could be driven as far as possible in a straight line. So each man held his land in the form of long thin strips. The village worked two or three Great Fields (survivals of the system are still to be seen in one or two places, such as Braunton Great Field in North Devon), each field being made up of the strips that belonged to individual people. They looked like giant patchwork quilts of corduroy, ploughed into the ridge-and-furrow surface that still corrugates many of our fields today. The system varied from area to area, but a typical arrangement might have worked as follows:

Field One Sown in the autumn with winter corn, to be harvested the following summer. The field was then rested or 'left fallow' the following winter, its weeds and natural growth being grazed by village animals which manured the soil with their dung.

Field Two Left fallow in winter, sown the following April with oats, barley, beans, peas or vetches. The barley would go for baking and brewing, the oats for animal feed or porridge, while the other three crops would replace nitrogen in the soil while growing and feed livestock as well.

Field Three Left fallow for a whole year; grazed and dunged in winter, ploughed in each of the following four seasons, sown with corn in October.

Each year all the strips were reallocated. Everyone had a share of good and bad land through this method, and everyone had the benefit in turn of the work of all his neighbours. There was also common

Offa's Dyke Heritage Centre, West Street, Knighton, Powys, Wales. Exhibition, housed in old school buildings, covering history and topography of 80-mile (129-km) Dark Ages earthwork of Offa's Dyke, and story of development of Offa's Dyke long-distance footpath. Audio-visual room; library. Riverside park, planted with many native plant species, contains section of the Dyke. Youth hostel attached; excellent base for exploring Offa's Dyke and 120-mile (193-km) Glyndwr's Way long-distance footpath, which starts here.

Chiltern Open-Air Museum, Newland Park, Chalfont St Giles, Buckinghamshire. Museum of buildings through the ages – barn, forge, granary, cottages, shepherd's van, wooden privy, etc – all saved from demolition. On-going project recreating three-field system, ploughing and harrowing with horses and sowing early strains of wheat by hand. Iron Age house with fields growing dye plants and flax; live 'Celt' as host.

land for the grazing of individually owned animals and poultry – and, of course, there was the forest, where pigs fattened on beech mast and acorns, and from which came the wood for building, fencing, firewood, tool-making and so on.

In their efforts to secure land for themselves, the early Anglo-Saxons expanded the boundaries of their settlements up the sides of the river valleys and out over the ridges until they met the neighbouring village's domains that approached from the opposite direction. Whole areas were entirely cleared of wildwood and brought into cultivation in this way. The memory of the widespread burning of forest that took place lingers in evocative place-names – Brentwood, Charfield, Burnley. Other place-names carry reminders of the Anglo-Saxon settlement activities that first brought them into being: Barwick (-*wick*, a cattle farm), Hurlingham (-*ham*, a flat pasture near a river), Warmley (-*ley*, a forest clearing or glade), Somerton (-*ton*, a settlement on open ground above a river), Piddletrenthide (-*hide*, a unit of land that could support a household – Piddletrenthide had thirty hides by the River Piddle).

THE VIKINGS

As the fighting and feuding gave way to settled farming in well-established kingdoms, the blocks of cultivated land made larger patches on the general green background of the forest. Then came the Vikings, who crossed the North Sea at the end of the eighth century and in the following decades burned and raided their way to domination of three of the four Anglo-Saxon kingdoms – Northumberland, Mercia and East Anglia. Blood was spilled in every corner of Britain once again; farmland reverted to forest as the Anglo-Saxons fled from the advancing Danes. Over in Northern Ireland tall round towers began to appear in the landscape, built by the monks to preserve their treasures (and themselves) from the enemy. The only effective resistance to the invaders was in the West Country, where King Alfred of Wessex succeeded in holding on to his marshy strongholds around Athelney in the Somerset Levels. Alfred forced the Danes into defeat with his great victory at Edington in 878. But the raids, the contested sovereignty and the farming and forest clearance that was continually started and then abandoned continued for another two centuries. The Norsemen themselves settled much of northern and eastern England, establishing towns like Leicester, Stamford and Nottingham. They settled agricultural areas, leaving their mark in such place-names as Barnby (-*by*, a farm) and Armathwaite (-*thwaite*, a clearing or meadow). Slowly and intermittently the clearance of the wildwood continued and the villages with their Great Fields advanced further into the wilderness. By the time the Normans landed on English soil in 1066 – the last invasion that Britain was to experience and the longest-lasting in its effects – only about one-sixth of the countryside was still under its immemorial green forest covering. ❧

Jorvik Viking Centre, Coppergate, York. 'Time car', with taped commentary, takes visitors back to Viking times and through reconstructed streets and houses of Viking settlement excavated on adjacent site, with authentic sounds and smells; then through site of original excavation. Gallery of objects found on dig.

THE NORMANS

William the Conqueror's great record of his new possessions, the Domesday Book of 1086, shows that the British countryside was well under cultivation, although the high and hard lands of Scotland, Ireland and Wales were virtually untouched and the wildwood forest still flourished in many places. Parts of the wetlands of the Somerset Levels, Romney Marsh and the Fens had been drained and reclaimed, but much of the marshland still went under salt water at each new tide. The larger villages had their fields banked, walled and hedged into fairly regular shapes, having created them in planned programmes of forest clearance. But in other places, where individuals were working alone, the fields were few in number and shaped irregularly as they were won acre by acre from the forest. There was still plenty of open space in the countryside, although the fertile lands of East Anglia were becoming crowded. Norfolk and Lincolnshire each had nearly 100,000 people, while Suffolk and Essex had about 120,000 between them: altogether a quarter of the population of Britain.

King William was a determined ruler who would not be deterred in his efforts to achieve his personal ambitions. The Normans he led were descendants of the Norsemen who had settled in Normandy only a hundred years or so before their invasion of Britain, so they had knowledge and experience of conquest and settlement. Soon the remaining wildwood – that ancient mixture of lowland oak and ash, downland beech and highland silver birch – was attacked as never before. In two centuries most of it had been cleared. Yet Britain could show a greater acreage of tree cover than at any time since the Anglo-Saxons arrived. The paradox is explained by the Norman love of hunting, which caused successive kings to plant new royal forests, such as the New Forest in Hampshire, and to declare other areas of woodland sacred to the chase – for example, most of Berkshire and Hampshire, the whole of Essex, the Forest of Winchester that ramified and extended through Surrey, Sussex and Hampshire; the wide forests of Somerset, Dorset, Exmoor and Dartmoor; a great swathe of the Midlands from the Forest of Dean to Huntingdon, and the moors and northern wastes of Yorkshire, Lancashire, Cumberland and Northumberland. In Scotland, where the Norman kings had less influence, the great Wood of Caledon still covered much of the Highlands. Ireland was invaded by the Normans a century after their conquest of mainland Britain; but here, too, their influence was not so strong.

Not all the royal forests were made up of continuous tree cover. Some, like the south-western and Pennine moors, were forests in name but treeless in actuality. But Forest Law applied to all of them and penalties ranging from fines to blinding, outlawing and death awaited anyone who was rash enough to poach on the king's preserves.

Yet the humblest peasant, if he could raise the necessary money, could obtain a licence to cut into a royal forest for the purpose of reclaiming the land for agriculture. Reclamation was taking place in the marshlands, too, led by the monks who began to acquire great expertise in the building of dykes, banks and sluices. In the Fens the monks ran banks inland from the sea walls to drain the enclosed land and to render it fertile, and other banks were built out into the salt-marshes to convert them into freshwater marshes for grazing. The geometrical fen landscape of dead-straight walls and dykes, which is familiar to us today, developed centuries after these early medieval enclosures, which left a mishmash of curving walls and snaking watercourses as small sections were reclaimed wherever and whenever possible. During this period, some of the high moors were brought back into cultivation. Hardy lone farmers began to cultivate the acid wastes of Dartmoor for the first time in nearly two thousand years, winning their fields with tremendous labour. Farmers with the same spirit of individual enterprise pushed the limits of their cultivation a few hundred feet up the sides of the dales and moorland valleys of northern Britain and ran many miles of stone walls along the boundaries of their land.

These lone farmers were often freemen, working outside the mesh of interconnected obligations that supported the feudal system of social organisation. Most agricultural workers were part of a well-established system in which the chief figure was the villein, who worked his own strips of land when he was not labouring for the lord of the manor. Burdened with fines, taxes and tithes, beholden entirely to his lord, forbidden to buy or sell land, or even to move away from his home village, the villein could still take comfort from the sight of his own productive strips of land, his own chickens scratching in the village dust, his own pigs in the wood and his own cows on the common. And in an even worse position was the wretched landless serf, who had no rights or freedoms whatsoever.

As time went on and the population of Britain began to rise, demand for produce from the land also rose. Only a hundred years after the Norman Conquest, some peasants who understood the value of money began to hire themselves out to the lord of the manor strictly for cash and they paid their rents in the same way. As they cut their way deeper into the wildwood, and the pigs and cows ate and trampled the green new growth of the forest, so new fields were created; and a new type of farmer, who was more independent than hitherto of the lord and his system-enforcing bailiffs and other henchmen, came into existence.

Wool became enormously profitable as populations both at home and on the Continent continued to rise, together with their demand for clothing materials. The wildwood that remained on the downs was gradually cut down and sheep began to graze the land. The country entered a period of increasing prosperity from sheep and woollen cloth manufacture, which was mirrored in its beautifully built and decorated timber-framed guild halls, 🎍 merchants' houses and churches. The Cotswold wool men beautified their

Merchant Adventurers' Hall, Fossgate, York. Timber-framed hall of York Merchants' Guild, built in 1350s. Timber posts and roof; exhibition of merchants and Guild history.

wolds with the creamy native oolite limestone. All over Britain towns began to spring up, some with a guardian castle and fortified walls, many as market towns growing on the site of a fair or market that had been granted to the local community by the king and encouraged by the lords of the manors for the wealth they created. Monastic communities, prospering on sheep production, introduced new landmarks into the countryside – towers, spires, grange barns, abbey churches and enormous monastery buildings that covered many acres.

THE BLACK DEATH

The Black Death plague, which was brought into England in the summer of 1348 by fleas living in the coats of black rats, swept through Britain for the rest of that year and throughout the warm months of 1349. No one was safe. Serf, villein, bailiff, lord, bishop or prince – anyone might find the hard little lumps in the groin, which were swiftly followed by black spots, raving, vomiting of blood, writhing, unconsciousness and death. From lumps to death might take less than one day. The Black Death killed perhaps as many as one person in three.

Within a decade, however, the wool trade was flourishing once again and the lot of the villeins – that is, those who had survived the plague – was better than it had been before. This renewed prosperity was due to the fact that there were fewer people to share the animals and fields, and the shortage of able-bodied men on the land meant that the peasant could sell his labour to the highest bidder. Some peasants became 'franklins' who rented with their own money land that they hoped to add to and improve on their own account.

The depopulation caused by the Black Death had a devastating effect in some parts of the country. It led to the abandonment of hundreds of villages, to the reversion of hard-won moorland and hilltop fields to forest or bog; to farm animals roaming the countryside at the mercy of the first person to find them; to the death of entire communities. The outlines of many abandoned plague villages may still be traced in the ground: a green ditch that winds with the contours of a hill and was once a village road; rectangular banks in a field that were the walls of houses; churches and manor-house moats in fields on their own, well separated from a village that was built in the years after the plague. But the gradual dawning of 'peasant power' and the realisation by the landowners of the impossibility of progress without the willing co-operation of their men, signalled the end of the feudal system. For agriculture in a depopulated countryside the best answer was sheep. Sheep were content to graze the marginal land, needed care and attention from one individual only and were certain to be profitable. Many fortunes were made from sheep in the centuries after the Black Death, but many people found themselves evicted from their villages and fields as landlords turned their land over to sheepwalks. By the

Abbey Barn, Somerset Rural Life Museum, Abbey Farm, Chilkwell Street, Glastonbury, Somerset. Early fourteenth-century barn of home farm of Glastonbury Abbey. Magnificent stonework and timber roof.

Alfriston Clergy House, Alfriston, East Sussex. Timber-framed house built for parish priests c1350. Two-storey Great Hall. First building acquired by National Trust (in 1896) after heroic, lone seven-year battle by vicar to save it from demolition.

Grey Abbey, Strangford Lough, Co Down. Impressive ruins and fine memorials of Cistercian monastery founded in 1193.

Cosmeston Medieval Village, Lavernock Road, Penarth, South Glamorgan, Wales. Excavations, open to public, of medieval village deserted after Black Death. Display of finds. Some reconstruction of buildings is planned for the future.

Medieval Yorkshire cruck house, now in Ryedale Folk Museum.

(Opposite above) This building at Snowshill was enriched by Cotswold wool.

(Opposite below) Ludlow Castle defends the Shropshire town.

(Right) A Cotswold building also enriched by Cotswold wool – North Cerney.

Guildhall, Lavenham, Suffolk. National Trust building; superb example, built in 1529, of ornately carved, timber-framed Tudor Guildhall. Exhibition of medieval building and wool trade.

The Old Grammar School, Church Lane, Ledbury, Herefordshire. Early Tudor (1480–1520) wool merchants' Guildhall which became Ledbury's Grammar School. Now houses Heritage Centre. One of large number of fine timber-framed medieval buildings in Ledbury.

Hezlett House, Liffock, Castlerock, Londonerry. Thatched seventeenth-century cruck house. Walk route through the building and its roof space to show how the timber cruck trusses support the structure.

turn of the sixteenth century there were lovely stone churches, manor houses and barns all across the English landscape, along with the new towns that were making inroads into the remaining wildwood. There were also vast areas of upland sheepwalks on which no peasants were seen; and armies of beggars – former agricultural workers who had been dispossessed and forced to roam – wandered the land.

FROM TUDOR TO GEORGIAN TIMES

From Tudor times onward the cutting of the forest continued apace. There was the wooden-walled navy to build to defend the country against the Spanish and the Dutch. As the population rose, more houses, more tools, more furniture and firewood were needed. As the three-field system of agriculture was replaced by bigger tracts of land owned by fewer individuals, so increased contact with other countries brought new crops into the new fields. Root crops like turnips could be fed to animals throughout the winter, enabling farmers to keep their stock alive from year to year and to abandon the established practice of killing the majority of their animals at the onset of winter when there would be a shortage of grass and forest food. More animals survived to fertilise more land with their dung and to allow more crops to be grown. Clover and trefoil were planted and the practice of silage and hay-making was fully established. Dye plants were introduced, too, to service the wool industry: madder for red, saffron for yellow. French Huguenots, fleeing religious persecution at home, settled in East Anglia and elsewhere in Britain, bringing their weaving skills and prosperity.

Turbulent Ireland had been devastated by Tudor military expeditions, launched to put down a series of rebellions. In Stuart times the north of the country was 'planted' with Scottish and English settlers, whose influence on the landscape was enormous and longlasting. They built roads, cleared trees and created farms, villages and towns very much like those on the mainland. These Presbyterians and Protestants were given the best land to work: the dispossessed Catholics were pushed back and up into the marginal hill country, boggy and stony land that resisted efforts to tame it.

This activity on the land devoured the wildwood at an everincreasing rate, covering the lowlands of Britain in fields and the uplands in sheepwalks. Across the moors and along the ridges spread a network of muddy winding packhorse roads and droving tracks along which the cattle, sheep and geese made their way together with the horseback bales of wool to market or port. The landscape of Britain changed decade by decade as landowners became more influential and the smallholders and landless labourers lost their holdings in field, common and heath. Parliament had always resisted the idea of the large-scale enclosure of land, but towards the middle of the 18th century the demands of the landowning class became too insistent to be withstood. So began the final moulding of the countryside into what remains its shape today.

ENCLOSURES

From about 1750 onwards, parliament's privately promoted Enclosure Acts permitted fields and heaths that hitherto had been held in common ownership to be hedged or fenced into smaller units for agricultural use. The intention was to allow everyone who could prove ownership a fair amount of land, in proportion to the acreage over which he or she had had rights before the enclosures. But in practice the rich, the forceful and the literate took all the available land, while those who could not claim ownership in writing or support their case in a court of law received nothing.

The scale of the enclosures was staggering by any reckoning. Between 1750 and 1850 about 4½ million acres (2 million ha) of open field were enclosed – this was roughly half of the available arable land, the rest having already been enclosed – and about 2 million acres (800,000 ha) of the existing 7 million acres (3 million ha) of common and waste land. The big open fields that had survived from the old three-field system, striped like corduroy with the different colours of their crops, some of them several hundred acres in size, were parcelled into small rectangular fields of 10 or 20 acres (4–8ha) each and were bounded by hedges. About ¼ million miles (400,000km) of hawthorn hedges were planted during these years, most of which were on the Midland farmlands that had hitherto escaped enclosure. Suddenly the countryside looked smaller, neater and greener – a satisfying sight to those with an increased stake in the land, but heartbreaking for the small farmers at the lower end of the scale who had been manoeuvred out of business. Some took to rioting, petitioning parliament and burning hedges and hayricks, but they had no hope of turning the tide.

Many of the dispossessed found themselves on the emigrant boats to the colonies of the New World alongside their Scottish counterparts, the clansmen who were being evicted during the Highland clearances of 1750–1850 as those great tracts of high country were converted into vast sheepwalks by their rich new owners. Already shattered by the savage penalties meted out to them after the bloodbath defeat of Bonnie Prince Charlie at the Battle of Culloden in 1746, the clans dispersed all over the world. They left behind them a land where stone-built houses crumbled into the bracken, where the ruins of once-thriving villages stood in the shadow of fine new gentlemen's residences, and where thousands of acres lay empty of all human influence – as they continue to do today.

At the same time the landed gentry and nobility were planning their estates, hiring the most skilful landscaping experts such as Capability Brown to implement their ideas. Landscape gardeners moved hillsides, created lakes in valley bottoms and built follies to give drama to far vistas. In some places entire villages were cleared and resited if they spoiled a landowner's view. Estate owners also began to plant woodland – hunting coverts and spinneys to encourage game, oak and beech woodland to build the navies of the future

Superb example of a tithe barn at Abbotsbury in Dorset.

Monastic splendour at Tintern Abbey in the Wye Valley.

Harmony between buildings and landscape at Luccombe, Somerset.

Medieval wool wealth built Kersey in Suffolk.

Stourhead House, Stourton, near Mere, Wiltshire.
Stourhead Pleasure Grounds: *jardin anglais* (mixture of art and nature) laid out 1740s–60s, extended later. Classical and English landscapes blended. Lake, temple, grotto, Pantheon, ornamental bridges. Thousands of tree and shrub species from all over the world. Booklet guide to a tour of the grounds; tree list available.

Hergest Croft Gardens, Kington, Herefordshire.
Gardens begun 1867 and developed ever since. Pleasure garden around Edwardian Hergest Croft house with magnolias, azaleas, lilies, roses, hydrangeas; also maples and birches. Kitchen garden with floral beds and borders. Park Wood: valley full of rare trees and huge variety of rhododendrons (some 30ft (9m) tall).

Tollymore Forest Park, Newcastle, Mourne Mountains, Co Down.
Arboretum begun over 200 years ago – hundreds of species, including wild strawberry tree, Monterey pine, sequoia. Also forest trails, viewpoints, café. Exhibitions in restored eighteenth-century barn.

Castle Ward, Strangford, Co Down. Eighteenth-century house with classical west front and Gothic east front; fine collection of trees and shrubs; formal gardens; wildfowl collection; information centre.

and to provide the coppice wood everyone needed, and more exotic foreign trees for their aesthetic appeal. For a time the planting of new woodlands kept pace with, or even outstripped, the continuing destruction of the ancient forests.

Meanwhile, the surge in agricultural improvements gathered momentum. New machines were invented for the efficient working of the new land – for example, Jethro Tull's seed drill of the 1720s and the cast-iron ploughshares that were developed by the family firm of Ransome's in 1785. Crops were improved by cross-breeding the best varieties to eliminate weaknesses, while cows, sheep and pigs were also improved by genetic engineering. Hundreds of thousands of acres in the fen country of East Anglia had been drained and reclaimed during the seventeenth century with the expert help of Dutch engineers. Now, with the enclosure of the rough grazing heathlands in Suffolk, Norfolk and many other parts of the country, corn began to grow in places that had been considered unalterably barren by previous generations.

During the last years of the eighteenth century and the first years of the nineteenth, the Napoleonic wars generated a great demand for food and clothing, which added to the boom in agriculture and the need for more and more land that could produce better and better crops. With the coming of the Industrial Revolution and the growth of the insatiably hungry manufacturing cities, it seemed that the farmers' prosperity was assured. The countryside had been cultivated and forced into full-scale production – but hard times were just around the corner.

THE SLUMP

As soon as the Napoleonic wars had ended in 1815, the price of corn and of wool plummeted. Farmers, who had enjoyed a period of great prosperity, found themselves facing the same rents, taxes, rates and tithes as before, but with assets that had halved in value during the course of a year and were due to halve again the following year. A great agricultural depression gripped the country. Many farmers went bankrupt; others let a proportion of their land go out of production, reduced wages to a minimum or made their labourers redundant. With common lands enclosed, poor people could no longer fall back in hard times on their own cows for milk and cheese, or on their own hens for eggs or pigs for bacon. The price of bread soared in the years immediately after the Napoleonic wars, because the Corn Laws, which were passed by the government to protect suffering farmers, laid down that the price of corn had to rise to 80s a quarter before cheaper foreign corn would be imported into the country.

Rootless, moneyless, homeless and without the means of supporting themselves and their often very large families, many redundant farm workers were forced to beg or to steal alongside the demobbed veterans of the Peninsular campaign and Waterloo. The Poor Law Amendment Act of 1834 at least put in place a framework for dealing with such unfortunates. Parishes throughout the land were grouped into Unions, each of which had to maintain a workhouse in which poverty-stricken but able-bodied persons of all ages could earn the 'bitter bread' of charity by sheer hard work. That same year the six Tolpuddle Martyrs were sentenced to transportation for trying to form an agricultural trade union.

The plight of the poor was not ignored by everyone from the more privileged classes, however. People from all strata of society resented the Corn Laws, which provoked such anger over so many years that they were repealed in 1846. The workhouses, too, were known to be grim, miserable places where families were separated and epidemic disease was rife. The workers were far from supine under their troubles; there were riots and rick-burnings afresh, and nocturnal smashing of the new agricultural machines that were supplanting labouring hands in field and farmyard. But British peasants had no political power. There were no votes as yet for the working classes. They were powerless in the face of such misery, fighting in futile ways a tide of history that was sweeping away their role in the world, as it swept away the last remnants of the medieval countryside which had endured for nearly a thousand years.

Nevertheless, although the rights of the common man were temporarily in abeyance and fear of mob violence was strong in the land, the fortunes of agriculture soon enjoyed an upturn with

Fife Folk Museum, The Weigh House, Ceres, Cupar, Fife, Scotland. Pre-mechanisation implements from Fife's agricultural past, displayed in seventeenth-century tolbooth and weigh house, and adjoining cottages. Also displays of Fife crafts and trades, traditional cottage interior, dolls and toys.

Shibden Hall Folk Museum, Godley Lane, Halifax, West Yorkshire. Hand and horse tools of bygone Pennine farming. Plough, seed fiddle, rake, scythe, shears, etc; also dairying equipment, horse-drawn vehicles, shops and sheds fitted up for traditional trades: clogger, saddler, blacksmith, wheelwright.

Packhorse Bridge at Allerford, Somerset, wide enough for a laden horse.

Norfolk wind pumps kept the reclaimed fields dry.

A haymaking party in prosperous pre-1914 days.

the increasing demand from the manufacturing towns. Farmers who did stay in agriculture entered a golden era of prosperity in Victorian times.

INDUSTRIAL TOWNS

The expansion of towns that developed as a result of the Industrial Revolution had an even greater effect on the landscape than the enclosures in areas where coal, iron and running water coincided. In the mid-eighteenth century, although industry was established in the cloth-making districts each side of the Pennines and in the iron-working areas of the Black Country, it was still a small-scale and local affair – a shed in the back garden from which to conduct business and a couple of acres of land on which to grow crops or vegetables or to graze animals for the table or nearby market. Industry and agriculture went hand in hand, but they were soon to be torn apart and would never join in partnership again.

Manor Farm, Upper Hamble Country Park, Botley, near Southampton, Hampshire. Working farm based on Victorian practices. Many farm animals, shire horse; bygone implements and machinery used and demonstrated; farmhouse and cottage garden; forge and wheelwright's shop. Rural celebrations. Regular demonstrations and events.

Northfield Farm Museum, New Aberdour, Fraserburgh, Grampian, Scotland. Large collection of farm equipment including tractors, implements, stationary engines, household bric-a-brac from 1870s.

Somerset Rural Life Museum, Abbey Farm, Chilkwell Street, Glastonbury, Somerset. Abbey Barn. Abbey Farm buildings and farmhouse: displays of nineteenth-century Somerset rural life. Farmhouse interiors; waggons and farm equipment; museum theme trails (eg farm history, farm machinery). Large programme of events all through the year, from Cider Apple Roadshow to Pole Lathe Bodging.

Ironbridge, Shropshire, where rushing water, coal and ironstone formed the foundations of the Industrial Revolution.

Weaver's House and Highland Tryst Museum, 64 Burrell Street, Crieff, Tayside, Scotland. Tartan handloom weavers, spinners and cordwainers, working in row of eighteenth- and nineteenth-century weavers' houses, producing textiles for sale. Big Scottish clan and family archive: over two thousand tartans recorded.

New Lanark, Strathclyde, Scotland. One of the world's largest cotton mill settlements, built 1780s onwards near Falls of Clyde, and site of Robert Owen's mill workers' co-operative community. Enormous mill buildings, stores, counting house, school, Institute for the Formation of Character, workshops, managers' and workers' houses: all restored, many lived and worked in. Craft workshops; Heritage Trail.

National Waterways Museum, Ellesmere Port, Cheshire. World's largest collection of traditional narrowboats. Displays in boat cabins; boat restoration; exhibition of canal life.

National Waterways Museum, Gloucester Docks, Gloucester. Displays telling story of inland waterways. Working models, films, demonstrations. Blacksmith; horses. Narrowboats, dredger and other craft.

Robert Owen Memorial Museum, Broad Street, Newtown, Powys, Wales. Display tells life story of Robert Owen, eighteenth-century industrialist and social reformer, Utopian visionary, pioneer of infant education, founder of co-operative communities, leader of mass trade unions and campaigner against evils of Industrial Revolution factories.

The rush of water that powered Richard Arkwright's spinning mill at Cromford in Derbyshire in the 1770s and Arkwright's and David Dale's mills at New Lanark in the next decade, was soon drowned under the hissing and puffing of steam power. Steam brought undreamed of prosperity to the mill and factory owners and to the building speculators who were rapidly developing the new towns. It also brought unheard of misery to the thousands of agricultural workers – some were dispossessed, others were desperate for a change in their circumstances – who flocked through the factory gates to take up lives of degraded slavery amid landscapes that rapidly changed from the delightful to the hellish. Anywhere where water rushed or coal outcropped might suddenly become a manufacturing centre from which the meanly built, lightless terraced houses, free of all sanitation, sprawled out into the countryside, which was polluted and fouled, blackened by smuts, scarred with canals, roads and railways, and heaped with ashes or colliery spoil, its colours hardening from the greens and browns and blues of nature into the greys and blacks of mechanised industry.

Hundreds of square miles were defiled in this way – around Manchester and Wigan, and between the cotton towns of Lancashire and the old wool towns of Yorkshire which were now swelling with heavy industry. And along the Tyne and in the Durham coalfield the shipyards and coalpits proliferated, as did their wastes and their ugliness. The green valleys of South Wales blackened; so did the blue skies of Staffordshire over the Potteries. As for the iron works of the Black Country, Elihu Burritt in 1868 viewed the devastation from Castle Hill in Dudley as follows:

Nature has the under-hand, and from the crown of her head to the sole of her foot she is scourged with cat-o'-nine-tails of red-hot wire, and marred and scarred and fretted, and smoked half to death day and night, year and year, even on Sundays. Almost every square inch of her form is reddened, blackened, and distorted by the terrible tractoration of a hot blister. But all this cutaneous eruption is nothing compared with the internal violence and agonies she has to endure. Never was animal being subjected to such merciless and ceaseless vivisection. The very sky and clouds above are moved to sympathy with her sufferings and shed black tears in token of their emotion.

Their yawning mouths ever ready for men, women and any children who were old enough to stand and guard a machine, the 'dark, satanic mills' became terrible symbols of the power and might of the Industrial Revolution, and also of its greed, destruction and disregard for human life and happiness. Most colliery and mill owners and ironmasters, who at first were proud to build their fine houses and lay out their private parks within full view of their creations, soon moved to more congenial rural surroundings, leaving

Lanark Mills on the Clyde, a Utopian experiment in industrial co-operation and better working conditions.

Castleford Colliery, Yorkshire – a hellish landscape.

the wretches of the manufacturing towns to struggle as best they could, along with those few selfless priests, doctors and practical missionaries who came to live and work side by side with them. Into the fever-ridden courts and terraces with their sewage-polluted wells, miles of poisoned ground and complete absence of greenery, sank a generation that had been born in the rural environment of a medieval landscape.

Within a few decades most city workers' natural affinity with the countryside had been expunged – as it had to be if people were to survive and remain as sane and as healthy as possible in such monstrous surroundings. The countryside was a place from which food came and into which one might venture a few times a year. The workaday world was as far removed from that experience as it was possible to imagine. The vagaries of the weather, the cycle of the seasons and the cranky customs of rural Britain meant nothing in Preston or Liverpool, in Glasgow, Pontypridd or Belfast.

One can trace from this period the deepening divide between town and country dwellers which has led to so many of the countryside's problems today – the farmer's hostility to the rambler, the car-load of rubbish that is dumped in a country lane, the overcrowded beauty spot and the surly holiday-village shopkeeper. There was a general view that natural resources were there to be exploited; that if ruination and defilement of the countryside was

The monstrous surroundings of the Industrial Revolution.

the price to be paid for progress and prosperity, then so be it. Many people expressed regret at the destruction of well-loved scenery; but of awareness of an ecological kind, of the interdependence of man and all nature, there was hardly a glimmer. Man was the master and he should play a masterful role.

Increased industrial production brought an enormously increased use of the country's natural resources. When Queen Victoria came to the throne in 1837, the coal mines of her kingdom were producing fewer than 30 million tons a year. By the time that she died in 1901, ten times that amount was being dug, with the attendant effects on the landscape.

At the time of the Great Exhibition of 1851, a third of Britain's industry was still powered by water; but only twenty years later, nine out of ten factories and mills were operating by steam, which was so powerful, efficient and reliable, yet so smoky, dirty and productive of foul waste. Steam power enabled a mill owner to build his plant well away from the river and its falls and weirs; the railways, with their ability to carry coal any distance, meant that he could move outside the immediate area of the coalfield.

The industrial South and West Ridings of Yorkshire and the eastern manufacturing area of Lancashire soon crept away from their original sources of power and gradually sprawled towards each other until only a narrow corridor of Pennine moorland kept them apart. In Northern Ireland, Belfast became a mighty shipbuilding and heavy engineering centre, while textile factories producing Irish linen proliferated in many other towns and country areas. And from all these factories, mills and iron foundries came flooding the well-made, inexpensive and reliable goods which earned Britain full coffers and a worldwide reputation, while her colonies poured raw materials into the mother country's docks and ports.

AGRICULTURAL DEPRESSION

For farmers in the late nineteenth century, the years of prosperity were followed by years of poverty on the remaining agricultural land. After what came to be known as the High Farming Age in the mid-Victorian era, there were disastrously wet summers at the end of the 1870s, followed by outbreaks of both crop and animal diseases. At the same time, the American and Canadian farmers made cheap wheat available. The price of English wheat, blighted and scarce as it was, fell sharply. The post-war depression of the 1820s was repeated. As before, some farms suffered financial collapse, while others let their land go out of production, reduced wages or made their workers redundant. The unfortunate agricultural labourer, who was always overworked and lived in conditions little better than those of his city-dwelling counterparts, found himself once more on the edge of destitution. By the turn of the twentieth century, fewer farm labourers were employed in the countryside than ever before – only just over 10 per cent of the population still worked in agriculture, compared with about 70 per cent in 1800.

Beamish North of England Open Air Museum, Beamish Hall, Stanley, County Durham. England's first open air museum. Visit drift mine of c1913 with contemporary buildings, engines. Pit ponies, steam locomotives and winding gear; pit cottages furnished in character. Also railway station c1910; Victorian market town with shops, pub, factories and a foundry, cobbled streets, bandstand, trams. Home Farm; transport collection. Beamish Hall: exhibition of traditional items and changing ways of life.

Yorkshire Mining Museum, Caphouse Colliery, New Road, Overton, Wakefield, West Yorkshire. Tour of coal mine workings 450ft (137m) underground. Exhibition of coal mining from 1800 to present day. Pithead baths, workshops, coal screening building. Nature Trail from colliery site.

Lady Victoria Colliery, Newtongrange, Lothian, Scotland. Pithead tour of renovated Victorian colliery. Introductory display in Visitor Centre: life in Scottish pit village as seen by Victorian miner. Self-drive 'coal heritage trail'.

City Museum, Weston Park, Sheffield, South Yorkshire. Story of Sheffield's evolution. Big steam engines. Range of products made in Sheffield, from plain table knives to a silver-plated penny-farthing bicycle made in 1879 for the Russian Czar. Photographs and display of effects of heavy industry on Sheffield and its landscape.

Landscape devastated by coal mining.

War brought relief to the farming community as it brought ruin to many a business and death to many a household. More wheat, more meat, was the cry as World War I drowned Europe in its lakes of mud and blood. U-boats were stalking the undersea waterways, and the convoy system had not reached the effectiveness of World War II. Some downland went under the plough as farmers grew crops to the limit of their capacity. After the war, the pattern of a hundred years before repeated itself – a Corn Production Act in 1918, intended to have exactly the same effect as the Corn Laws, suffered precisely the same fate of unpopularity and eventual repeal in 1921; and the ensuing slump, which was exacerbated by the general recession in world trade in 1930, lasted until World War II. This was the time so directly and movingly described by A. G. Street in his book *Farmer's Glory*. Imports of food rose to 70 per cent by the outbreak of war, while thousands of acres became derelict. Farmers yet again had to make stringent economies, reduce their workforce and in many cases sell their farms. Sad landscapes of thistle fields, tumbledown barns and overgrown hedges became a common sight.

FORESTRY

Another great change in the landscape between the two world wars came about as a result of the government's determination that Britain would not be caught drastically short of wood, as it was in 1914. Although the rich landlords of the eighteenth and nineteenth centuries did plant a good deal of woodland all over the country, tree planting had steadily declined throughout Queen Victoria's reign. Iron had replaced timber as the chief shipbuilding material; coal was used for domestic and industrial fuel rather than wood, and coke had replaced charcoal in iron-smelting.

As with farming, the low price of timber offered by the colonies, and by Scandinavia, made the importation of cheap softwoods (coniferous tree timber) an attractive proposition. By 1914 only about one in twenty of Britain's acres was under forest, and almost all the country's pit-props, wood pulp and deal planking were imported. When blockades were introduced and the demand for timber soared in 1914–18, home-grown wood was not available. Over a third of all the woodland in Britain had to be cut down during the four years of war, and afterwards the Forestry Commission was set up to make sure that it never happened again.

The Forestry Commission bought up more than a million acres between the wars (becoming in the process the biggest landowner in Britain) and planted them with conifers. The corduroy battalions marched over the Scottish and Welsh hills and borders, down the spines of Northumberland and the Lake District, over the sandy heaths of the Breckland of East Anglia. At first they were planted as unrelieved conifers – dark green rocket shapes by the hundred million, a harsh, dull and alien-looking covering. But by slow degrees the Forestry Commission learned about breaking up outlines and about planting hardwoods (broadleaved trees) along the margins of the great sombre forests to soften their appearance and to give them some seasonal variety. In this way, great tracts of hitherto marginally productive land assumed a glory of usefulness if not of appearance.

Thetford Forest Information Centre, Santon Downham, near Brandon, Suffolk. Forestry Commission display on Thetford Forest: planting, management, felling, wildlife, walks, camping, etc. Information, books, leaflets, forest tours.

But accurate forecasts for the future use of such a long-term crop as timber usually turn out to be only guesswork. The most mature of the new softwood trees were only twenty years old – sixty to seventy years being their optimum felling age – when Europe went to war again in 1939. As had happened a quarter of a century before, a massacre of the remaining wildwood and private woodlands took place, and one third of the remaining trees were cut down. By 1945 Britain was looking pitifully short of its traditional broadleaved trees, although there was no shortage of conifers.

MODERN AGRICULTURE

The agricultural landscapes, too, had undergone further upheavals during the war. Any land that was not already used for arable farming came under pressure to grow crops. In the grimmest days of 1940–1, when the U-boats had the upper hand in the Atlantic and

Corduroy battalions of conifers have
over-run many Scottish hillsides.

The battalions fall to the power saw.

Britain was conducting a lonely defence, much of the downland sheep pasture that had survived the ploughing of World War I disappeared under corn, as did more commons, marginal land and pastures. The lawns of some great country houses, the pride and joy of their head gardeners, were ploughed and sown for the few extra acres of crops they could produce. Chemical fertilisers were used widely, increasing yields generally and reducing reliance on the natural manure of farm livestock. Fed with artificial concentrates and silage, cattle no longer needed to be kept on the land for as many months of the year as possible. The indoor rearing of calves, pigs and hens began to be introduced, the forerunner of today's battery farming techniques.

Most significant of all as agents of change were the tractors, sent by the United States across the Atlantic in increasing numbers, which began to supplant the cumbersome steam-driven machines that had been in use since mid-Victorian times. Hedges were ripped out, ditches were filled and copses were cut down to smooth the path of the tractors and their clumsy equipment. And the farm horse, that steady and trusty worker on whom men had relied so heavily for so many centuries, began to lose his central position in the farming scene. In 1940 he still seemed a fixture, an indispensable lynch-pin in the agricultural world, his disappearance unthinkable. Twenty years later he had all but vanished from the countryside, along with the lumbering iron machines he drew and the skills and lore of twenty generations of horsemen.

So the modern age began.

Maldon District Agriculture and Domestic Museum, 47 Church Street, Goldhanger, Maldon, Essex. Collection of tractors and farm implements salvaged or donated locally.

Norfolk Shire Horse Centre, West Runton Stables, West Runton, Cromer, Norfolk. Shire horses working daily: demonstrations of harrowing, ploughing, rolling, harvesting, etc. Display of role of horse in agriculture. Ponies, small animals, rural collection.

Galloway Farm Museum, New Galloway, Dumfries and Galloway, Scotland. Display of horse implements from early nineteenth century onwards. Demonstrations of farm horses at work on cultivation and harvesting of oats, hay, turnips, potatoes. Horse-and-cart rides.

Traction engine and tractor: the old and the new.

The patient farm horse, always at the centre of operations until World War II.

The new techniques that were introduced during the war took firm root and the countryside was never to be the same again. With modern chemicals, the British arable farmer found that he could spray away many of the problems that had plagued his forefathers for generations. Insecticides would kill the aphids, the worms and beetles that infested his crops. Fungicides would destroy the mildew, rot and scab. Herbicides would clear his fields and hedgerows of weeds. Fertilisers would impregnate his soil with nitrates and phosphates, enabling him to dispense with the traditional rotation of crops and periods of fallow, allowing him to concentrate on one immensely productive crop – potatoes, barley, wheat, or whatever best suited his situation. Modern machines would gather the hundredfold harvest effortlessly into the barns.

The dairy farmer saw his herds fatten on artificial concentrates, on silage and on grass that had been chemically stimulated to a richness his father never knew. The beef farmer fattened his calves likewise – carefully cross-bred productions from Friesian mothers, artificially inseminated with sperm from Hereford or Aberdeen Angus bulls – by artificial light in artificial indoor conditions. Pig farmers followed the same road to greater production and prosperity. Egg producers no longer had to hunt around the hen-houses and straw stacks of the farmyard for the day's offerings: they could be picked from under the little wire cages, tier upon tier, in the battery houses without losing a single one.

But the natural law that lays down a minus for every plus cannot be sprayed or dosed away. Along with the technological improvements have come a host of troubles. Those chemicals that promised

Central Museum, The Strand, Derby. Derbyshire Nature Gallery Project: 'The Nature of Derbyshire' exhibition. Impact of man on landscape of Derbyshire from earliest times to present day. Features models of typical Derbyshire farm of 1930s and same farm today, showing loss of hedges, woods, meadows, wet places and other wildlife habitat.

to eradicate the pests and the weeds, the diseases and the impover-ished soil, have bred such resistance in their target foes that they have had to be continually reinvented and updated. Meanwhile, chemicals have had a devastating effect on the wildlife of the coun-tryside. Songbirds, wild flowers, fish, water plants; voles, field mice, butterflies, hawks; foxes and stoats, hares and hedgehogs – all have had their numbers decimated by agricultural chemicals. The giant wonderful harvesting machines roar their way through vast tracts of East Anglian prairie landscape devoid of hedges and ditches. The Friesian dairy herds give milk that is thin and tasteless compared with the creamy nectar that grandfather knew. The same is said of today's beef and pork, which are produced from animals whose constricted lives stir pity and indignation in many human hearts. And as for the battery hens, insanely pecking their cages and each other, riddled with disease and terrified of natural light – how can they be expected to deliver eggs that are anything but pale and insipid?

For these modern evils of farming there are remedies, most of them unpalatable to the farmer in the short term because they involve a loss of profits and an increase of labour, and they also increase prices for the consumer. If organic farming ever gets a proper toehold, the countryside might return to the richness of natural life. Farming without any modern chemical or mechanical aids is probably viable only for the dedicated few, but many farmers have proved that it is possible to run a financially sound operation hand-in-hand with the conservation of wildlife. Several of the farmers who are featured in Chapter 3 are setting an excellent example in this respect.

The chief victim of all these changes appears to be the modern farmer himself. A good deal of the farmer's traditional pride and pleasure in his job has disappeared with the advent of today's farm-ing methods. The mixed farm, which demanded his involvement in every aspect of the business and lent interest and variety to his work, has all but vanished. No longer can the farmer see himself concerned chiefly with the quality of his produce, refusing to hurry a job that needs to have time spent on it. Producing for the giant supermarket chains, he has to combine both quality and quantity as his forefathers never did. It is more difficult to work in tune with nature and the seasons. Too often the farmer finds himself fighting nature just because the necessary chemical or technological weap-ons are readily available.

The long, low, forbidding farm buildings, too, overloaded with concrete and plastic, stand marooned in the midst of the farmer's fields, unarguably out of place and out of sympathy with their setting. Modern services of mains electricity, gas and water have enabled him to live at the heart of his operation; but he lives alone, outside the village community that enclosed and sustained his ancestors' dwellings. Nor does he have the companionship of the twenty or thirty farm workers whose hands and intelligence were

needed constantly at every point of his grandfather's farm. His machines can do all that for him, a hundred times more efficiently, even though machines make cold companions. Today's young farmer, shut away in his tractor cab, his Walkman plugged in under his ear mufflers, often seems a lonely figure in an empty, if profitable, landscape.

The farmer of the late twentieth century – a lonely figure in a profitable landscape.

THE COUNTRYSIDE TODAY

In the last fifty years the British countryside has seen many great changes outside the world of agriculture. On the negative side must be ranged the ravages of open-cast mining and quarrying; the insidious and ever-increasing sprawl of building in new towns, new village developments and urban growth; new roads that have pushed through irreplaceable landscape on what appear to be the slimmest of excuses; the pollution of rivers and other waterways with sewage and industrial effluent; the churning up of ancient trackways by motorbikes and off-road motoring clubs; and the needless construction of theme parks and amusement centres on land which developers may see as barren and useless, but which naturalists know to be the home of wildlife that has nowhere else to go.

On the positive side can be counted the enormous increase in public awareness of ecology, of natural history and of the fragility and fascination of the whole interdependent world of nature; the snatching of wetlands, woods and other wild places from the jaws of developers and their safeguarding in the hands of wildlife organisations; the establishment of the national parks and nature reserves; and the reinstatement of landscape by the mining, quarrying and pipe-laying concerns that disturbed it. These changes in the countryside are explored more fully in Chapter 4.

The recently exposed prospect of change in the landscape that has been brought about by the 'greenhouse effect' of global warming may yet see the most far-reaching changes since man began his tenancy in this world; equally, he may achieve a more profound shift in his habits than he has ever done, and thus avert the threat. Time will tell.

Tempting though it is to look back nostalgically and view the pre-war scene as a golden age and every change that has happened since as a change for the worse, the perspective of history shows our contemporary alterations in the life and appearance of the countryside as only the latest – if in many ways the most rapid and far-reaching – in a chain of change that has been jerkily unrolling since the geological bones of Britain were first laid down. For every swing there has been a roundabout; for every downturn, there has been an upswing, and inevitably this has been followed by another downturn. Certainty of change has been, and continues to be, the one abiding characteristic of the British countryside.

Lyn & Exmoor Museum, St Vincent Cottage, Lynton, North Devon. Wonderful, packed and jumbled mass of items – pictures, farm implements, kitchen equipment, peat-cutting tools, domestic gear – giving strong flavour of changes in Exmoor life and work over the centuries. Idiosyncratic labels and odd exhibits only add to delight of this unique museum.

CHAPTER 2

WILDLIFE IN THE COUNTRYSIDE

The eel had obviously been trying to reach the open water below the salt-marsh. It had wriggled a winding course for thirty yards through the fleshy leaves of the sea purslane and now lay stiffened in the silvery carpet half way between creek and muddy shore, stabbed clean through by the heron that had stopped it in its tracks. Already the glutinous sheen of its skin had dulled to a steely grey and the exposed rib bones were dry and brittle. The heron stood sulkily on one leg on the shingle bank above the creek where he had flown from his prey, his feathers ruffling in an icy wind, watching and waiting for me to finish my inspection of the eel. Further along the shingle a pair of oystercatchers circled above their nest with fast black-and-white wingbeats and piped furiously from their long orange bills. They need not have worried – it would have taken more than a dead eel to keep me on my knees for very long, with the April wind whipping bursts of sleet across these dark, dour Essex marshes.

Britain can show a greater number of habitats for wildlife than almost any other land mass of comparable size. It is a richly endowed country where (with a certain amount of forthright driving!) you can stroll before breakfast among the Mediterranean flowers and palm trees of Cornwall, take a mid-morning break watching a herd of Exmoor red deer on the skyline, lunch in the garden of a pub in a mid-Wales valley in whose woods red kites are nesting, hear curlews piping over the Pennine moors in the afternoon, lie on a grassy sward in Upper Teesdale in the early evening among heavenly blue spring gentians and other relics of Ice Age flora, and be crouched on the rocks of a lonely sea loch on the west coast of Scotland as the sun sets, with a family of otters frolicking on the tideline before you. Each of these landscapes – salt-marsh, clifftop, moorland, mountain, limestone upland and seashore – is only one piece of the complicated jigsaw of natural history that is Britain. None of these landscapes would be complete without the others to complement it. Each has a wildlife, not exclusive to it alone but characteristic of that landscape, which has endured through the centuries. What added warm enjoyment to that bitingly cold April walk in the Essex salt-marshes was the thought of the same life-and-death drama between heron and eel being played out on the same piece of ground under the gaze of Victorian naturalist, medieval wildfowl trapper and Saxon fisherman, all of them roundly cursed in the same piping tones by a pair of agitated oystercatchers.

A dedicated and expert natural historian could happily spend a lifetime studying one acre of ground anywhere in Britain, and at the end of his life – and what a wonderful life – still be ignorant of nine-tenths of what had been taking place right under his nose. The oak tree whose life he had come to know as well as his own would still be a mystery to him, with its birds, its insects, its leaf galls and bark fungi, the voles that burrowed among its roots, the squirrels that leaped among its branches, the hidden tides of its sap and the ever-changing patterns of its unfolding buds, falling leaves and bare winter twigs.

This chapter does no more than touch on some of the wildlife that the observant but inexpert watcher might hope to see in a selection of habitats in the countryside of Britain. For every bird, tree, plant, animal or insect that you are lucky enough to spot in a hedgerow, on a mountainside or by a river, you can be sure that there are a hundred more getting quietly on with their own business, some of them within view but operating their well-tested methods of staying unseen and unmolested, others hidden away under stones, behind grass clumps or in the branches overhead.

The average walker in the countryside, on opening a book on wildflowers or birds to learn something about what he is likely to see, feels a sense of inferiority grow with every page he turns. How can he ever hope to gain that smooth certainty that the writer displays about the difference between the early purple and the marsh orchid, or tell sparrowhawk from kestrel with absolute confidence in the split second when the bird flashes across his path? The answer is that he cannot, without a great deal of study and day-to-day fieldwork – and it doesn't really matter. The thrill comes with seeing wildlife in action all around you and with the occasional but intense satisfaction of matching the rough guess of the moment with confirmation from the book as you sit at home in the evening, massaging your blisters, with a glass that cheers at your elbow.

This is not to say that you should necessarily lighten your pockets by leaving the flower or bird book at home when you set out for a day's ramble. The well-known Sod's Law states clearly that the day you do so is the day that it just might have been a corncrake you heard in the meadow, or a clump of spearwort that was growing by that marshy stream – and now you will never be sure. The main point is to get out in the open and enjoy what you do see, from the rarest to the most commonplace, whether your walking territory is mountain, moor, limestone upland, chalk downland, pasture and meadow, arable farmland, hedgerow, woodland, heath, wetland, riverside, estuary, marsh, cliff or shore. In that order we will take a wildlife walk, working with the geological grain of the country from the high to the low, from the bleak to the lush – although there is little bleaker in Britain's landscape than an Essex salt-marsh in sleet.

MOUNTAIN

Mountains, of course, mean heather. From mid-summer to early autumn the springy twigs and tiny purple flowers are crunched

Kendal Museum, Station Road, Kendal, Cumbria. Lake District Natural History Gallery: views into different Lakeland habitats on 'nature trail' around a series of dioramas: mountain, forest, lowland, etc.

'The blooming heather.'

underfoot wherever you walk in the mountains, perhaps following one of the narrow dry paths that have been trodden bare by sheep. Many people think that heather looks at its best, however, when October turns it to a deep fiery orange, especially when it is contrasted with the dark green of Scots pine and the black of the highest peaks of bare volcanic rock. Bell heather, with larger bell-shaped flowers of a darker purple, grows where the conditions are drier, often on higher, more exposed shoulders of mountainside. Earlier in the year, from May onwards, the pink flowers of bilberry – 'blaeberry' in many parts of Scotland, 'bleaberry' in the Lake District, 'whortleberry' in the West Country – grow in carpets of bright green small leaves among the heather and in the pine woods of moors across Britain. Bilberry pie and local cream is a delicacy from

Cumbria to Dartmoor. Sabine Baring-Gould had a nice account of it in his *Book of Dartmoor* (1900):

> A gentleman from London was visiting me one day. As he was fond of good things, I gave him whortleberry and cream. He ate it in dead silence, then leaned back in his chair, looked at me with eyes full of feeling, and said, 'I am thankful that I have lived to this day.'

In sheltered crevices high in some British mountain ranges can be found colonies of rare arctic-alpine plants such as alpine meadow rue, mountain sorrel and purple saxifrage, still surviving at these unfrequented and unpolluted altitudes ten thousand years after the last Ice Age when they flourished all over Britain.

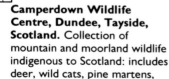

Cwm Idwal National Nature Reserve, Glyder Mountains, Snowdonia, North Wales. A glacier-hollowed corrie with cliffs that shelter arctic/alpine plant communities.

In *Journey Through Britain*, John Hillaby wrote of the Scots pine: 'It has about it the quality of a bugle blast.' Scots pine can grow to 100ft (30m) and more, a straight, slim trunk of rough bark that is cracked in long vertical plates and tops out in a bushy crown. Pitch, resin and turpentine were extracted from Scots pine, and its timber was used for masts and spars when Britain's navy had wooden walls; as a result of its practical use and the centuries of clearance and burning, there are only a few tattered remnants of the countless millions of Scots pine that once formed the great Wood of Caledon that covered Scotland. A faint whiff of that departed glory can be caught on the remote mountain slopes of Wester Ross, where there are enough of the native trees left to flavour the landscape. Other mountain trees are the slender silver birch with its slim trunk which is blotched with black and the palest grey, and the rowan, or mountain ash, which produces sprays of white flowers in spring and bright red berries in autumn.

Above the 1,500ft (450m) mark in the highest and loneliest mountains of west and north Scotland, or over the basalt crags of Skye and the other west coast islands, are the only places you are likely to spot the great wings, steady as a plank and ending in outspread fingers of feathers, that carry the golden eagle. Contrary to legend, golden eagles do not take crofters' babies off to their eyries, and if they do steal the occasional lamb it is usually one that is sickly and unlikely to survive anyway. But in spite of their low numbers and protected status, a few farmers still put out poisoned carcasses to destroy the birds; and egg-robbers home in on the nests with the dollars of unscrupulous egg-collectors in their minds. Somehow the golden eagle clings to its strongholds in the mountains, although its numbers fall from year to year. Most sightings of golden eagles turn out to have been of buzzards, their rounded wing-tips and smaller outlines having been widened and enlarged by wishful thinking. If you hear a cat-like mew or a whistle, it is the cry of a buzzard.

Camperdown Wildlife Centre, Dundee, Tayside, Scotland. Collection of mountain and moorland wildlife indigenous to Scotland: includes deer, wild cats, pine martens, golden eagles, buzzards.

Ravens and crows are also commonly confused by birdwatchers in the mountains. Ravens are not as rare as golden eagles, so you may well see the big shape of one overhead, with a great heavy head

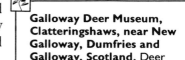

enlarged by a massive black axe of a bill – a bigger and heavier bird altogether than the crow. The raven's call, which is often echoed by its mate in the rocks below, is a deep bark or burp, a grating sound like a very old motorbike on a cold morning.

Red deer are far more often read and dreamed about than seen. For such a big animal – the biggest stag can stand the height of a man or more at the shoulder – they can melt into complete invisibility among heather and rock. Walking on the island of Jura in the Inner Hebrides and knowing full well that at least five thousand red deer were there somewhere with me, I spotted only one group of about fifteen, glimpsed for a few seconds as they stood watching me tensely, before turning tail and trotting over the skyline.

When planning a walk in the Scottish hills, it is as well to check on the time of year. From July to the following February is the deer-stalking season and a careless incursion into shooting territory during those months can easily end with a bawling-out by an enraged stalker, if not with the sudden arrival of a more permanent discouragement from the rifle of one of his clients.

Mountain hares are much more rarely seen than their lowland cousins; your best chance is probably early in the year when the landscape has reverted from white to brown, and some mountain hares may not yet have followed suit in changing their white winter coats for the brown pelt of summer.

Feral goats – those that live wild all the year round – can be spotted in craggy places where coastal or inland cliffs provide those ledges, inaccessible to their enemies, on which the goats move along as nonchalantly as if they were on a wide meadow. In the Mull of Oa, at the south-western tip of the Isle of Islay, I once saw a herd of feral goats run full tilt away from me and over the edge of a 300ft (90m) cliff. Appalled at my responsibility for this apparent mass suicide, I hurried up to the cliff edge and peered over, to see the goats calmly nibbling grass 200ft (60m) below me on a ledge not wider than a bookshelf, each animal outlined against the sea, a sheer drop above and below them. How they achieved that descent in less than a minute – how they got down there at all – I cannot imagine.

MOORLAND

The acid peat moors of Britain, which were cleared of their wildwood during man's early attempts to tame and exploit his surroundings, have presented a forbiddingly empty and sterile face to the explorer for thousands of years. There is nothing more depressing to the eager rambler as he starts out in Derbyshire on the great 250-mile (400-km) adventure of the Pennine Way than to find a thick mist clinging clammily to the sodden, squelching, empty brown back of Kinder Scout. Dartmoor, even on a sunny day, can strike cold shafts of unease into the heart of any walker with its long featureless swells of ground that seem to block the view ahead as if deliberately, in which wildlife appears at first sight sullenly unapproachable, if not entirely absent.

Moors repel the intruder with their uncompromising deadness of appearance, their tremendous silence which is not the majestic, timeless stillness of mountains, but an absence of noise that feels as if it springs from an absence of life. Man has experienced only a string of defeats in his battles to make things grow on moors. Barren and negative places they may seem, baked dry by sun or soaked into quagmires by rain, but they are far from dead. Heather and bilberry, raven and red deer are inhabitants of moorland as well as mountain.

Where water wells from underground or collects in a boggy dell from the slopes of the ground, you can find mosses ranging from black velvety cushions to the bright green sponge of sphagnum moss, which takes your descending boot in a gentle embrace that quickly becomes a clinging, sucking restraint to further movement. These waterlogged places are often covered in the white feathery flowers of cotton grass that looks exactly as if soft down has been scattered in handfuls.

Northern Ireland is more intensively farmed than the rest of Ireland, but there are still many thousands of acres of bogland. The ombrogenous or rain-fed raised bogs, growing in constricted sites and forced to swell upwards, and the outward-spreading blanket bogs are rich in plants. Butter-yellow whins (the Irish term for gorse) grows on the boglands, along with purple masses of wild rhododendrons. Closer to the ground are the white-flowered Irish lady's-tresses orchid and the sticky, insectivorous sundew. Wales, too, has extensive bogs in its mountainous areas which support many plants, birds and insects. Other British plants include the white cluster of heath bedstraw and the pink flowers of lousewort, whose top petal curves down over three pendulous lower ones like the wattles of a farmyard cock.

A spicy smell like rich fruit-cake, wafting across moorland on a hot summer day, may drift your way from a clump of juniper. It grows in the form of bushes at high altitudes or, in certain wind-scoured locations, as a flat ring of miniature leaves; but further down the contours it may straighten and sprout up to the size of a small tree, bearing berries that vary in colour from smoky green to smoky blue, its leaves spiky and evergreen. A strong sniff of juniper brings exhilaration to the rambler on the dullest moor.

The bubbling liquid call of curlews is another moorland delight. Plump and speckled brown, the curlew probes soft ground for invertebrate food with its slender, downward-curving bill. The moors are its chief stronghold for spring and summer rearing of chicks in nests among the sedges and coarse grass, although in winter many birds shift to the muds of estuaries for the lugworms and small soft-shelled creatures buried there. The cry of a curlew, which is beautiful and mournful, never fails to tingle the hairs on the back of my neck. It catches perfectly the feeling of moorland.

Hooded crows make a less attractive sound and their tastes are equally degraded. Birds of the Scottish and Irish moors and farm-

Tregaron Bog National Nature Reserve, Tregaron, Dyfed, Mid-Wales. Raised bog on a former lake site. Plants include deer grass, cotton grass, heather, cowberry, bog rosemary, cranberry, bog mosses, sundew. Forty species of breeding bird. Buzzard, sparrowhawk and red kite as well.

lands, their grey backs and hopping walk are red rags to bullish crofters and farmers who shoot them out of hand at lambing time. 'Hoodies' are particularly partial to the eyes and tongues of new-born lambs.

Red grouse are shot as well, but their habits are not the cause. Whether it is their flavour on the table or their value as one unit to be counted towards a big total of kills for the day, is open to question. The grouse have a lean time anyway, without those hard-paid-for lead pellets. They die in their thousands from parasitic infections, which in bad years make the renters of grouse moors wish they had put their money into gold mines instead. Grouse feed on heather and fires can decimate their numbers. No wonder they rise explosively under your feet and whirr away on stubby wings, shrieking 'Go back! Go back!' in hysterical voices. I would do the same if I were a grouse.

Smoky blue juniper berries give out their fragrance on a hot day.

LIMESTONE UPLAND

Naturalists have good reason to love the airy uplands of Britain which are bedded on limestone. Coming from the bare grandeur of the moors to one of those great rolling sweeps of grassy hills and lush valleys, all the hard work of seeking out something to delight the eye is instantly behind you. Where peat is merely channelled and bogged by flowing water, the soft limestone rock is cut, hollowed and scooped into terraces, slopes, cliffs and valleys. Here water is a sculptor given free rein with a most responsive yet durable material, and its masterpieces include the fantastically shaped pinnacles and buttresses of Dovedale in the Peak District, the wild green dales of Yorkshire and the Cotswolds' rich valleys and long rounded hills.

The greatest glories of the limestone uplands are their wild flowers. The acid in the soil is neutralised and its bite made toothless by the calcium carbonate of the limestone rock underneath. Bacteria can live in such soil, breaking it down to release nutrients which feed the wild flowers and which acid peat can never supply. To walk down from the lonely peat moors above Cauldron Snout waterfall into the pastoral peace of Upper Teesdale, where the same tiny, brilliantly coloured flowers have been growing for the ten thousand years since the last of the ice sheets receded, is to walk from ecological famine into a land flowing with floral milk and honey.

Upper Teesdale is admittedly a very special case, a refuge for those sub-arctic flowers that have vanished from almost every other part of Britain. The best known is the spring gentian, so startlingly, royally blue that you can hardly believe your eyes when you see it. The spring gentians have become rarer in recent years with the spread of herbicides and other pollutants and with the increase in visitors to Upper Teesdale hoping to spot them. Older folk in the area tell you of the blue drifts of gentians that they remember from their young days; but now the locations of the little clumps that remain have to be carefully watched and warded by conservationists. Other survivors of that delicate flora of the tundra are the yellow and purple mountain pansies and the bird's-eye primrose, whose purply-pink flowers with a yellow spot in the centre grow in a cluster from the top of one stalk in the manner of a cowslip.

The cowslip itself is a fast-disappearing species. Gone are the carefree days when country people picked them by the bucketful to make a heady wine or to treat their bronchitis. Overpicking has drastically reduced their numbers, as has their sensitivity to agricultural chemicals and the dairy farmer's switch to artificial feeds from the traditional cattle grazing and dunging of meadows which encouraged cowslips to grow. You will most likely spot them in spring in small clusters on the edges of woods or on remote, steeply sloping hillsides; also on one of man's own creations, the disused railway line, where they are left undisturbed to suck in nutrients that have been washed out of the limestone ballast left behind on the abandoned trackbed.

Primroses, on the other hand, are still relatively common in springtime under hedges, in woods and on the banks of country lanes. The primrose is a tough little flower and adaptable enough to cross-breed with garden primulas that have escaped into the wild. Ironically, the garden primula, which is descended from the wild primrose, is now helping to enrich its parental stock and to spread a fine range of colours into natural surroundings.

A plant that is very characteristic of the limestone uplands is bird's-foot trefoil, its tiny leaves forming a mat on which are dotted the bright orange-yellow flowers whose top two petals meet in a domed peak like a Spanish conquistador's helmet. Buttercups do well on limestone – can you remember the first time one was held under your chin to see if a yellow reflection betrayed a passion for butter? Knapweed thrives here as well, its flower like a purple shaving-brush in the same shape as a thistle's. The two are often mistaken for each other at a casual glance, although knapweed has no prickles. High on the sides of fells and hills above the farmlands grows tormentil, a tiny yellow flower with four petals in the shape of a Maltese cross. Where one tormentil grows, you will generally find a thousand. On a sunny day you can treat yourself to a nose-tingling scent of herbs if you crush the white, rounded flower-head of yarrow between finger and thumb. Yarrow's leaves are dark green and narrow, feathering outwards from their central stalk.

The flowers mentioned here are only a random selection from the commonest of the many floral treasures of the limestone uplands. My personal favourite is a solitary harebell trembling in a breeze at the end of its slender stem, its bell of a flower the subtlest shade of milky blue.

The great broadleaved trees of the farming countryside generally find the soil too shallow and the winds too strong for survival on these open uplands, but you will often come across bushes and clumps of hazel bearing nuts which some people think are at their most delicious when eaten green and milky in the half-ripe stage.

Blackthorn bears the round purple-black sloe berries in late autumn. Chewed in the raw, they make the inside of your mouth thicken and crawl as if you were eating blotting-paper that had been dipped in bitter aloes. To get the best out of sloes, pick them after the first frost of the winter has taken the floury bloom off them. Prick them a few times with a needle, half fill a bottle with them, add an inch or two of white sugar, top up with gin and wait (if you can), turning the bottle every couple of days until the sugar dissolves and the gin flushes a deep ruby red. Then go for a very long walk and get as cold, wet and miserable as you can. Return home and sit by a fire and pour your first glass of sloe gin, after which you can abandon all thoughts of any further activity for the rest of the day. For such hours God made the blackthorn.

Of all the small brown birds you may spot flittering from stone to grass and back to stone again, the one most easy to identify – and the one most likely to enliven your limestone ramble from start to finish – is the wheatear. From early spring to late autumn the

The primrose, still a common springtime flower.

wheatear bobs, skims and flutters in the loneliest of the uplands as chirpily as it does along the most frequented of the long-distance footpaths. Its song is a chittering, scratchy sound. What distinguishes the wheatear from the other small brown birds is its white rump, which flashes unmistakably against a green and grey background and which gave the bird its name. That charmingly rural name is derived from a nickname that was bestowed on the wheatear by countrymen who were long on accurate observation if short on poetry – 'white arse'.

CHALK DOWNS

Chalk downs are as rich in lime as limestone uplands, but the chalk in its greater softness weathers into quite different and distinctive shapes. In the classic chalk downland country of Dorset, Wiltshire, northern Hampshire and Sussex, the hills have been moulded by wind and rain into a smooth roundness. In their sides, the meltwaters of interglacial periods scooped out dry valleys, but the heart of these billowing hills is solid chalk, many hundreds of feet deep. Viewed from a good distance after they have been freshly

Wild thyme spices the downland air.

ploughed so that the whiteness of the chalk lies on the surface, a succession of Dorset downs resembles a row of sails that have been laid flat and bellied upwards by some great wind blowing up into the sky from underground. They seem to strain at their moorings in the valleys below. Walking on these tops on a breezy day is, in fact, rather like sailing – the racing clouds, the springy downland turf that bounces you from step to step, the bursting plumpness of the downs curving away and down on both sides as if in motion themselves. It lifts the spirits as few other forms of walking do. Downland walking has inspired some of the very best writing, too – prime examples are *Wildlife in a Southern County* by Richard Jefferies, *Nature in Downland* by W. H. Hudson and *The South Country* by Edward Thomas.

Part of the exhilaration of walking across the downs has to do with their smell. Wild herbs grow thickly in the turf that has been cropped short by sheep, releasing their fragrant smells as they are crushed by your boots and warmed by the sun. Wild thyme and wild marjoram in particular give a spicy undercurrent of scent to a walk on the downs. Milkwort, a short plant with a thin thread of stem up which the tiny blue flowers grow alternately on this side and that, is often seen, as it thrives on short turf and lime.

If you are lucky and observant, you may spot two unusual orchids, the spider orchid and the bee orchid. The markings on their lower petal, the largest and most pendulous one, look like the rear ends of the insects that give them their names, pushing into the centre of the flower.

Self-heal, a bushy and fuzzy-looking flowerhead that is studded with blue flowers on dark green leaves, is also a characteristic downland plant. Betony, which grows on the slopes and rims of the dry side valleys, is similar to self-heal but pinker and more upstanding. Another plant with a fuzzy flowerhead is devil's-bit scabious, whose tiny blue flowers have petals of papery thinness. In the verges of trackways that lead down to the cultivated land below the downs grow the springtime primroses and cowslips that also grace the limestone countryside.

Some of these downland trackways are thousands of years old, trodden out by men in times when for safety's sake any journey had to be made high above the dangers of the forests and bogs in the valleys, where animal and human enemies could be lurking unseen. Yew trees mark out the course of many ancient tracks across the downs, their dark green spiny foliage and gnarled, branching outlines being visible from far away. You may find a sizable grove of yews where two tracks cross each other, or on the site of a long-vanished inn where sheep and cattle drovers met to rest their beasts and exchange news and gossip over the cups. Yews were planted or left to grow where they had seeded themselves, as markers of such important places. They were held to bring good luck to the traveller, although they could deal death to any animal that was allowed to browse on the poisonous leaves or fruit stones.

The beech, which grows in long belts on a ridge to give shelter from the weather or in round spinneys on the crest of a hill, is seen everywhere on the chalk downs. Beech trunks are smooth and grey, and often grow to a massive girth of 30ft (9m) and more. Their roots spread sideways for many yards under the turf, knobbling the pathway where they break the surface. On both cold and hot mornings a steamy veil of mist hangs around the beech woods long after it has shredded away from the surrounding slopes. In wet weather they drip dankly, smelling of leaf rot and fungus. Beech trees are at their best on a sunny afternoon in summer when their canopy of leaves filters shafts of sun into a light that is half gold, half green when it reaches the ground in pools and spots.

The butterflies of the downs have been decimated since the advent of chemical spraying, but their numbers were already declining after the two world wars of this century when so many acres of downland sheep grazing were ploughed up for crops. The little chalkhill blue can still be seen where its main food plant, the yellow-petalled horseshoe vetch, is found growing, and the same applies to the marsh fritillary (which sounds as if it should be confined to the coasts of East Anglia) and its food plant, devil's-bit scabious. The bright yellow brimstone and the orange-tip frequent the hedges and banks of old trackways, fluttering in seemingly haphazard circles and zig-zags across the path, rarely coming to rest.

If the wheatear is the characteristic bird of the limestone uplands, the skylark is the familiar bird of the downs. Whether you start your walk at 6 o'clock in the morning or 3 o'clock in the afternoon, there will be a skylark somewhere overhead pouring out a stream of song as it climbs invisible, vertical stairs, hovering for a few seconds on each aerial landing before mounting the next flight. There is no pause in the song, however. Any operatic singer would envy the breath control of the skylark. Walking to the accompaniment of skylark song is one of those rare delights one never learns to take for granted; it is a fresh and keen pleasure every time.

Rabbits once infested the English downs like fleas on a hedgehog, but myxomatosis and ploughing have greatly reduced their numbers. Where the downs are still covered with short turf the rabbit burrows show as bald white holes with a shallow scrape in front, their round droppings spattering the grass nearby. The grassier parts of the downs and the grass fields below them are the main stronghold of the hare, whose British population has also been on the wane. William Cobbett in his *Rural Rides* tells of an incident in 1822 when he set out to prove that a farmer at Netheravon on Salisbury Plain could not show him and his companions a solid acre of hares, as had been claimed:

We went over the next day. Mr BEECH received us very politely. He took us into a wheat stubble, close by his paddock; his son took a gallop round, cracking his whip at the same time; the hares (which were very thickly in sight before) started all over the field, ran into a *flock* like sheep; and we all agreed, that the flock did cover *an acre of ground*.

Hares are not present in such abundance nowadays, but I have seen six or seven in the same downland field, all racing off as soon as they spotted me, then stopping all at the same time to crouch in a circle facing inwards. The hare is much bigger and redder in colour than the rabbit, and its ears are tipped with black. Its long hind legs provide the power for a fast, smooth running action as opposed to the rabbit's short, lolloping bursts of speed. Hares live above ground in a 'form', or nest, in the grass, and a quiet walker can often get within a yard or two of the animal before it jumps startlingly up and pelts away in a zig-zag dash. Its springtime mating and challenging rituals are famous as the boxing, leaping and sparring of the 'mad March hare'. The motives of people who bring dogs illegally on to the downs to course and destroy such a handsome, interesting and harmless animal are hard to fathom, to say the least.

GRASSLAND – PASTURES AND MEADOWS
Below the uplands and the downs, where the rich farming ground

widens out into the plains and valleys of lowland Britain, the dairying pastures and hay meadows spread their green grasslands. A turn-of-the-century farmhand would stare in wonder at the colour of some of those pastures today, an almost luminous green that owes more to chemical dressing than to rainfall and the muck cart. Even though the herds of black-and-white Friesian cows fatten better on the grass of such pastures than did the shorthorns that he knew, he would be saddened at the monotony of the green sward and its lack of wild flowers.

Fortunately, however, not all the flora has been entirely destroyed by chemicals. Damp areas of the grazing fields are spotted with blue where the cuckoo flower grows – a plant also known in different parts of the country as milkmaid, may flower and lady's smock. Its long stem is topped with a sprout of thin stalks from which the flowers droop their heads, as a shy milkmaid might do. The yellow, daisy-like flowers of ragwort also colonise these damp grassy places. Dandelions show their golden-yellow bursts of petals in pasture fields, and buttercups thrive here too, often covering several neighbouring fields and giving the milk of grazing cows (old-fashioned farmers will tell you) a special creaminess. The cows also do well on clover, both red and white varieties. Pick a bunch of clover petals and suck their lower ends to taste their sweet nectar.

Hayfields, like pastures, have been enriched with chemical fertilisers to the detriment of their wild flower populations, and the replacement of traditional scything by cutting with machines seems to have impoverished them in the same way. But orchid-spotters may well have a good day in the hay, finding the common spotted orchid with its pale pink or purple flowers dotted with dark red; or the fragrant orchid where the soil is rich in lime, a plant without the tarry leaf blotches of the common spotted variety, but whose pink flowers have a sweet clovery smell.

Hawthorn, or may, was the bushy tree most commonly chosen to form the hedges of pasture fields during the enclosures of the eighteenth and nineteenth centuries, and its strongly scented flowers whiten the grassland hedges in late spring as if they had been vigorously dusted with flour. Dark prickly holly grows in these hedges too, as do oaks, the nobly shaped, hardy trees that are most associated with the pastoral scene. Field maple can often be found growing to medium height among the oaks and hollies, its leaves shaped like a five-fingered hand.

Grassland butterflies include the brown family of skippers and the blue butterflies where the grass has been left to grow untouched for some time, especially in hayfields towards mowing time. Along the south coast of England, the clouded yellow makes unpredictable but occasionally spectacular invasions in early summer from the continental countries bordering the Channel. Clouded yellows gather in great numbers in the clover fields, mating to produce English broods later in the summer. Their wings are a dusty but vivid greeny-yellow – hence their name – with a

Cobtree Museum of Kent Rural Life, Lock Lane, Cobtree Manor Park, Sandling, Maidstone, Kent. Hay meadow planted with over eighty grasses and wild flower species to recreate medieval meadow rich in native plants. Traditional hay cutting and rick building. Also four-course rotation of crops; laid hedges; coppice and nut woods; herb 'knot garden'; orchard; hop garden; bees; Romney Marsh sheep; Sussex cattle; oast house. Craft demonstrations.

Doum Manor Forest Park, Cookstown, Co Tyrone. Butterfly garden, with flowering plants supporting a great variety of butterflies from larval to adult stages. Interpretation centre.

brown border to the upper surface and a white spot beneath, which is visible when the butterfly comes to rest on a plant and closes its wings.

Skylarks sing over the lower grasslands as they do over the downs, and both curlews and lapwings come down from the higher ground when the grass is waterlogged to probe for worms and insects. Lapwings nest in the open on the ground, their brown-blotched eggs superbly camouflaged; but you can tell when you are near a nest by the antics of the parents who scream their country name of 'pee-wit' as they dive-bomb you, sometimes clapping their wings together with an alarming crack. In the air they fly a dazzling aerobatic routine, tumbling and twisting towards the ground in a whirl of black-and-white wings that looks uncontrolled, until a few inches from the ground they suddenly regain grace and stability as they fly off. Their characteristic pattering, jerky run over the ground is a clever ploy, bringing inquisitive worms and insects up to the surface to discover what all the noise and vibration is about.

The haymeadows, with their abundance of mice and voles, make good hunting grounds for kestrels which hover patiently overhead watching for the slightest movement. Kestrels and sparrowhawks are the hawks most commonly seen on country walks and the most commonly confused. Over the meadows you are more likely to see a kestrel, whose wings are pointed in contrast to the rounded wing-tips of the sparrowhawk. The kestrel's body shape is more slim and streamlined and its tail projects in a long line behind.

You may spot a kestrel almost anywhere – in spite of lead poisoning of their blood from car exhausts, they have even succeeded in making good hunting grounds of the grassy verges of motorways – but you will probably have to travel to the wilder areas of Northern Ireland, Scotland and the Western Isles to hear, let alone to see, the once-common corncrake in its favoured hayfield habitat. Only in these remote places of small-scale farms, where traditional farming habits persist, do farmers leave the hay in the fields long enough for the corncrake to hatch its eggs. Corncrakes will nest in long grass in other locations, but seclusion and freedom from human interference are essential to the survival of this seldom-seen bird. If you do hear one, though, its call is unmistakable, for it croaks its Latin name *crex crex* with a rattling, grating sound. Corncrakes eat insects which the farmer would gladly do without, so their almost complete disappearance from mainland Britain has added to the woes of their chief exterminator.

ARABLE FARMLAND

Our turn-of-the-century farmhand, walking out of the pasture field and stopping to stare over a gate into the neighbouring field of corn, would be struck by the rich colour and the thickness of the crop and by the absence of these flowers which were so familiar to his generation – the poppies that he saw every summer spreading dots of red through the gold of the corn, the bright blue cornflowers and the big yellow daisyheads of corn marigolds. Today's rambler must travel to the remoter areas of Britain, to the Highland and island fields where herbicides are not yet so universally or enthusiastically applied, to find cornflowers and corn marigolds.

Poppies continue to make their appearance in the English cornfields, but their stronghold these days is at the margin of the fields where the chemical sprays fall more thinly. The poppy is a remarkably hardy flower, its seeds being capable of lying dormant under the soil for decades. An encouraging example of their capacity for resurgence was shown in the mid-1970s in the cornfields of the North Norfolk coast near Cromer. Here along the tops of the cliffs there had been such an abundance of poppies in Victorian times that the whole area had been nicknamed 'Poppyland'. But when the Norfolk farmers began to spray chemical herbicides the poppies disappeared. It was apparently a case of successful genocide. Visitors looked in vain for the famous poppies for the best part of fifty years, until the recession of the 1970s made spraying too expensive. Men with scythes returned to cut down the weeds of the cliff-tops – and back came the poppies, sprouting as vigorously as ever from seeds that must have been lying dormant in the soil for nearly half a century.

Charlock can also withstand pollutants, and the edges of corn, potato and cabbage fields can all be found splashed with the bright yellow of its four cross-shaped petals.

Hawthorn or may, oak and the sweet-smelling elder (whose flowers make light and heady champagne and its berries a dark and delicious wine) are typical trees of the arable farmland hedges. But the king of the trees, the dark and majestic elm with its spreading dome of foliage in an inverted cone shape, has all but vanished from the landscape – a victim not of agricultural chemicals, but of a fungus that is carried by a tiny beetle.

The classic farming scene, which has been painted and photographed so often, is of the ploughman and his team of horses overshadowed by a couple of towering elms. Elms stood not only in the hedgerows but singly or in twos and threes in the middle of the fields, casting a deep cool shade into which farm labourers throughout the centuries retreated to eat their midday meal. Elms' hard timber would make as durable a baby's cradle as it did an old man's coffin. Elm trees seemed an immutable part of the landscape.

But then came *Scolytus scolytus*, the European elm bark beetle, an insignificant-looking little creature about a quarter of an inch long with a black head and thorax, and brown wing-cases. There had been intermittent outbreaks of Dutch elm disease since the middle of the nineteenth century, but in the 1970s an infestation began that took far greater toll of the elms of Britain than ever the Black Death did of the human population. Within a couple of years the elms were dying where they stood in hedgerows and fields from the south coast of England to the Scottish border. Their bark dropped off like discarded armour, their leaves turned yellow and fell, and the ravaged, whitened skeleton of the trees raised bone-white arms to the sky until they were chopped down. Many of these skeletons still stand as pathetic reminders of the beauty that elms once gave to the countryside.

The course of the disease is very straightforward, perfectly understood by scientists and yet almost impossible to stop. The adult elm bark beetle alights on a tree and bores a shaft through the bark. The female usually does most of the work, while the male tidies the tunnelling debris away. Once they have bored under the bark, they excavate a chamber and mate. The female then tunnels away from the chamber, laying her eggs at intervals as she goes. As the eggs hatch out, the larvae dig their individual passages at right angles from their mother's tunnel, forming a pattern under the bark like the central body of a centipede with wavering legs sprouting outwards. These larvae, which are impregnated with the *Ceratocystis ulmi* fungus as their parents were, spread the fungus as they tunnel their way round the tree until they are ready to pupate. Then they stop, developing the hard shells from which in time the young elm bark beetles emerge to dig their way up through the bark to the outer surface of the tree. From there they fly off to begin the process all over again on some other unfortunate elm, leaving their host tree riddled with the fungus. The tree fights back against the infection by developing swellings or cysts in the channels along its trunk that carry water and essential nutrients up to the leaves. The cysts block the channels as blood clots block human arteries, the leaves die through lack of food, and the entire tree slowly starves to death, shedding leaves and bark as it does so. If you pick up a piece of bark under a dead elm, you can see on the underside the centipede-shaped patterns where the elm bark beetle larvae tunnelled and infected the tree.

Scientists have developed a virus which attacks and destroys the fungus, but as yet no method has been found of spreading it through large enough numbers of elms to affect the course of the disease. Individual elms can be treated successfully, but the cost is prohibitively high over areas of any size. The beetles and their larvae cannot survive very cold winters, but several severe winters in succession would be needed to eliminate Dutch elm disease on this scale, and those have not so far been forthcoming. Elm suckers, the slender sprouts of new trees, still push hopefully up each spring all over the country, but they, too, become targets for the disease as soon as they grow to any size. Perhaps in a few generations' time, the elms will begin to grow tall again, re-established to enrich the landscape by a scientific breakthrough, a run of miserable winters or the development of natural immunity. One can only hope.

Where crops are found – for example, grain, roots, kale, cabbage, peas, beans, sprouts – there you will find pigeons. They are not exactly the farmer's friend. The pigeon has an expandable crop or internal bag which it can easily fill every day with its own weight in food, and flocks of several thousand can descend on the fields of just one farm. Pigeons regurgitate the contents of their crop to feed their young in the form of a kind of thin vegetable soup, which thickens as the young bird grows until it is ready to fly off and persecute the farmer on its own account. Count the expended cartridge cases along the hedge to find out the size of any farmer's particular pigeon problem. They are shot in enormous numbers in the corn, on the stubble and over the vegetable fields, but they keep returning. Blessed with thick breast feathers, a tough constitution and an innate wariness which has them jinking behind trees and hedges as soon as they are on the wing, pigeons are the bird population's great survivors. They will probably outlast every farmer in the land.

Rooks are another of the arable farmer's blacklisted birds. They, too, eat grain, peas and beans, and congregate in big numbers where the food grows. They are easily distinguished from crows by the pale patch where their bills join their faces and by the ragged black feather 'trousers' on their thighs. They nest in raucous colonies in trees, choosing a favoured wood or spinney year after year. Along with their diet of marketable crops, they also eat a good number of insect pests, but they are still seen as much more of a foe than a friend. In the past, farmers would shoot young rooks with rifles to cull their numbers and take the carcasses home to be made into rook pie, but modern palates have become too discerning – or perhaps too dulled – for that old-fashioned country delicacy. Nowadays, they are scared off the crops, as are crows and pigeons, by mechanical 'guns' that fire a blank every couple of minutes. The first of these heart-stopping explosions you hear always seems to be the one right beside you. It is a horrible and frightening noise, but you can walk on out of range. One can pity the local inhabitants when the farmer forgets to turn the gun off at night. I write as one who has suffered at 3 o'clock in the morning.

On stubble fields you will often put up a flight of partridges, which skim off low over the ground, their plump bodies propelled at amazing speed by their short whirring wings. The common or grey partridge, which is hatched in broods of up to twenty at a time and adapted to grassland habitats, has maintained its numbers well. But red-legged partridges have declined since insecticide spraying wiped out much of their food source; they have tended to keep to the arable land on which they were introduced a few hundred years ago as sporting birds.

Man takes his lordly decisions and changes his agricultural practices as he thinks fit, and wildlife thrives or suffers in response – suffering being the more usual result. Since the introduction of silos to hold grain and open-sided, cheaply erected Dutch barns to store straw and hay, the solid old barn of brick, stone or timber has gone out of use in many areas, East Anglia being a prime example. Now these strongly made and attractive buildings sell for conversion to houses at enormous prices. The buyer gains a characterful house and the farmer a handsome profit. But the barn owl, once a familiar resident of farmyards, has declined in numbers to the point

When the chemical spraying stops, the poppies come back.

where it now appears near the top of the list of endangered bird species. The fall in numbers is due almost entirely to the demolition or conversion of its roosting places. When corn was threshed in the barn, the farmyard was alive with rats and mice feeding on the fallen grain, and barn owls had a plentiful supply of prey. Nowadays threshing takes place in the interior of the same enormous machine that gathers the harvest and the pickings for rodents – and therefore for barn owls – are far slimmer.

You may spot the brown figure with the white face of a barn owl standing motionless, probably asleep, in the shadows of a doorway or other opening high up under the roof of a disused barn of the traditional type, or be startled by its ghostly white form drifting across your path as you come towards the end of your walk through the cornfields at dusk. A more likely sighting will be of the small brown little owl, a nineteenth-century introduction from Holland that has spread through England and Wales. The little owl eats much the same diet as the barn owl, but also takes the occasional chick of poultry or game-birds. It roosts on tree stumps and fence posts as well as in barns.

Swallows and swifts can be seen around farmyard buildings at any time between April and late October, swooping to catch insects in mid-air and returning with a beakful to their thinly squeaking young in the mud nests that they attach under the roof beams of barns, sheds and even the farmhouse itself. But swallow numbers are falling too, as the African deserts continue their creeping spread and the birds that spend the winter there find fewer and fewer insects. Swallows, swifts and house martins are often confused – the house martin has a white rump and its forked tail is short, while the swift's wings, which are longer than those of either the swallow or the martin, carry it much faster through the air.

Little brown birds are likewise a constant source of confusion to the amateur bird-identifier. In the cornfields they may well be corn buntings which feed on insects and also the seeds of any hedgerow weeds that have escaped the farmer's chemicals. Yellowhammers will enliven any winter walk on stubble fields, darting out of the hedge in a sulphurous yellow flash or perching on a twig to chant their phrase 'A-little-bit-of-bread-and-no-cheese!'. And over the stubble, the corn and the farmyard hedgerows hangs the kestrel, awaiting his opportunity to pounce on mice and voles.

Although the threshed grain no longer lies scattered around barns and farmyards, rats and mice are still frequently seen on a walk in arable countryside. Harvest mice weave their nests between the stalks of corn, climbing up to eat the seeds in the ears on the top of the stalk. Moles are seldom above ground long enough to be spotted, although their hills of tunnelled earth are mounded in the fields. But rabbits, myxomatosis notwithstanding, still manage to become trapped in the cornfield as the harvester roars round and round, reducing the standing corn to a small refuge in the centre of the field seething with terrified animals. When the corn was cut by hand and there were twenty or more men at work in the field, a slaughter took place as the final stand was felled and the refugees dashed for shelter towards the hedges all around the edge. Nowadays people are not so hungry for a rabbit stew and the creatures are usually allowed to make their getaway. Many modern harvesters on fields of hundreds of acres in size work up and down the field, which leaves the last strip beside the hedge and lets the animals sidle away out of danger and unseen.

HEDGES

Hedges have been a part of the British landscape for a very long time. During the eighteenth- and nineteenth-century enclosures hedges were planted across the big open fields and commons to divide them up into neat little holdings.  Enough hedgerow was created in that hundred-year period to stretch from the earth to the moon. But the same amount of hedgerow already existed in the countryside, some of it dating back to Anglo-Saxon times – the word 'hedge' comes from the Old English *hege* or *haga*. *Hegeraewe* was a hedgerow and *cwichege* a living planted hedge rather than one made of cut branches that were piled onto the ground. Well before the birth of Christ farmers had seen the advantage of putting something discouragingly prickly between crops and animals. It was a logical step from piling up a barrier made of cut thorns to shaping one from the branches of thorns that had been planted.

Meikleour Beech Hedge, Meikleour, near Perth, Tayside, Scotland. Planted 1746. Now tallest hedge in the world – 100ft (30m) high, 1,750ft (533m) long. Some of its trees are over 120ft (36m) tall.

Some hedges were not planted deliberately but were kept as a strip-shaped remnant when a piece of forest was cut down, or were managed and nurtured from underbrush that had been seeded by bird droppings. Hedges have been shaped and controlled in much the same way from the Dark Ages to modern times. The stems – usually of thorns – were grown until they were considered sturdy enough, then cut half-way through near the ground and bent over at right angles or on a gentle upward slope. Their trailing stalks and thin branchlets were then woven around stakes that had been rammed into the earth between the hedge stems. The spikiest parts – thorns and twigs – were laid so that they faced the side of the hedge from which animals were expected to approach – a lane, a common or a patch of grazing. Some hedgers planted a supple sapling like hazel around the stakes. When it grew to the right height it was woven into a loose net to keep the top of the hedge in shape and to confine the animals. The new growth of each spring meant tidying, pruning and shaping work for yesterday's hedger, unlike today's machine operative who has only to steer his tractor straight and let the hedge-slasher rip and splinter along indiscriminately. It was worth looking after the hedges properly because they were so useful in such a variety of ways. They were boundary markers, deterrents for wild animals, protectors of crops from domestic animals, sources of firewood and field dividers.

The hedge beside which your footpath runs may be a thin screen of newly planted hawthorn, its soil still bare of plants and its twigs empty of birds' nests, or it may be a solid wall of foliage 3yd (3m) thick and over a thousand years old. A good rough-and-ready way to date a hedge is to pace out about 30yd (27m), counting the main species of woody plants that make up the body of the hedge. Every species in your measured length represents a hundred years' growth. So if you find, for example, hawthorn and elder, oak and beech, holly and yew in the 30yd stretch, your hedge might be as much as 600 years old. Hedges that were created during the great Georgian and Victorian enclosures tended to be of hawthorn only, which could be planted easily for miles at a time and guaranteed to grow both quickly and thickly. Those of medieval or earlier date have, of course, had longer to be colonised by a greater number of species and were planted initially with a bigger range, if they were not already more varied by virtue of their origin as part of the native wildwood.

Other useful hints that a hedge may be old are a wavering, wandering course where the centuries have caused changes in ownership or landscape; big stools (stumps of cut trees) several feet in circumference; stumps of major tree species which have been pollarded (cut off where the branches begin to sprout from the trunk) and the resulting shoots woven into the fabric of the hedge; the presence of holly, yew, spindleberry or wild service tree, all of which are likely to show medieval or even earlier date; and the supporting bank or base of the hedge full of plants such as bluebells, wood anemone and dog's mercury, which take many decades to establish themselves fully in hedgebanks.

Primroses and violets are classic hedgerow flowers in the spring, as both do well in shady situations. Also thriving in the shadow of the hedge is the lords-and-ladies plant, whose tall green 'leaf' – or, more correctly, spathe – encloses a spadix, or cylindrical purple spike, at the base of which grow the tiny yellowish-white flowers. After the spathe has withered away the fruit ripens, a spike of unmistakable orange berries that can cause extreme sickness if eaten. Thanks to its suggestive shape – male spadix within female spathe – lords-and-ladies rejoices in some fine earthy country names: cuckoo cock (Essex), dog's dibble (Devon), priest's pintle (Cumberland), stallions and mares (Lincolnshire), wake robin (Scotland).

In the grassy verges of hedges in any lane you will find the five bright pink petals of red campion growing on a hairy stalk, the big blue five-petalled flowers of meadow cranesbill and the little pink flowers, also with five petals, of herb robert. These last two have leaves with ragged toothed outlines, those of herb robert often looking more red than green. Jack-by-the-hedge has heart-shaped leaves with toothed edges like nettles (but shiny), white flowers and a penetrating stink of garlic. It, too, has a good variety of country names: garlic mustard, hedge garlic and sauce alone.

Everywhere along the hedgerow, and particularly in sunny lanes, grow the umbellifers or umbrella-shaped flowerheads such as cow parsley, chervil and angelica. They are bafflingly hard to tell apart at first, but with a few searches through the umbellifer section of the flower book the main types soon become distinguishable. Cow parsley is the familiar one, flowering from April onwards, whose hollow stem was once a favourite with children for making pea-shooters. Chervil flowers a few weeks later and the flowers grow on the ends of slender green stalks which all sprout out of the top of the same purple stem. Sweet cicely's seeds smell of aniseed if they are crushed. Angelica's flowerheads make a fluffy ball at the top of a tough purple stem. These all have tiny white flowers, unlike the yellow blooms of alexanders which grow near the sea in enormous numbers – the North Norfolk coast can show a mile or more at a single stretch.

The introduced and rapidly spreading giant hogweed is a sinister cousin of these benign plants. There is no mistaking the enormous shoots of giant hogweed that thrive in the damp ditch of a badly drained hedgebank. They can grow 15ft (4.5m) tall, with

Foxes find rich pickings among the wildlife of the hedgerows.

flowerheads 6in (15cm) or more across. In hot sunshine they develop a poisonous sting which has given many an unwary blower of a giant hogweed-stem pea-shooter a blistered lip or tongue.

You may, sadly, suffer other ill-effects if you try to eat blackberries that have been gathered from a hedge along a busy main road. Hedges absorb a great deal of air-borne lead and other pollutants from car exhausts, and their fruit can be foul.

Hedgerows offer some of the best shelter and nesting-perches a small bird can find, as well as plenty of fruits, seeds, nuts and insects. Small songbirds that are likely to be seen anywhere along a hedgerow include the yellowhammer, robin, blackbird, wren, and the dunnock or hedge sparrow with its celestial blue eggs that are laid in a clutch of three, four or five, to be seen either in the nest or in broken pieces on the ground under the hedge after hatching. You will probably spot pink-breasted chaffinches, too, or hear their sharp 'pink-pink' call.

Where small songbirds feed, there are the bigger birds that exploit them. The cuckoo's large egg, a pale, greyish-brown, may be seen in the nest among the blue eggs of the hedge sparrow, taking the place of one of the sparrow's own eggs that has been removed by the mother cuckoo. It promises a month's hard labour for the foster-parents as they try to keep up with the young cuckoo's enormous appetite. A sparrowhawk may suddenly dash over or along the hedgerow to grab some unfortunate small bird or mouse in its claw in mid-flight.

Black-and-white magpies dart around the hedges looking for unattended eggs to thieve.

> One for sorrow, two for joy,
> Three for a girl, four for a boy,
> Five for silver, six for gold,
> Seven for a secret never told

goes the old countryman's rhyme, and there are those (myself included) who automatically greet every solitary magpie they see with a 'Good morning, magpie' to avert the threatened sorrow.

Hedges offer as good shelter and food supply to animals as they do to birds. Hedgebanks were the chief burrowing sites of rabbits before myxomatosis and in recent years they have begun to be used again in the same way. Rabbits are not truly native animals of Britain – they were introduced in Norman times as a source of food and quickly became established as an extremely successful breeding species. They are hardy, quick, alert and very prolific – the doe can breed in her first year of life and produce up to five litters a season. Many rabbits are now of a strain that has developed some resistance to myxomatosis, but on any walk along a hedgerow or in grassland one is liable to come across a victim of this horrible disease, crouching in a miserable stupor with swollen, pus-filled eyes and dull fur. A sharp bang behind the head with a stick is the kindest and quickest end such sufferers can hope for.

Myxomatosis was introduced into Britain in 1953 by the Ministry of Agriculture as an experiment to control the rabbit population which then numbered 100 million or more, and which was nibbling away the profits of farmers up and down the land. As with the Black Death, the disease is carried by a flea, which only attacks rabbits. The experiment was effective beyond the wildest dreams of the Ministry scientists. I well remember as a child passing one stinking crouching furry body after another on a walk up Bredon Hill in Worcestershire when the unstoppable tide of myxomatosis was in its first flood. That familiar, well-loved family excursion turned into an experience full of horror that I shall never forget.

Rabbits that escape myxomatosis have a large number of animal predators to cope with. Hedgerows are good places to find stoats and weasels, little brown killers that always bring a shiver of menace whenever they are seen. Weasels, which are much smaller than their stoat cousins, prey on the mice and voles of the hedges, but it is the stoat that the rabbit dreads. Stoats can be seen standing on their hind legs, sniffing and looking around for prey. The stoat picks on one individual rabbit and hunts it down in disregard of any others in the vicinity. The victim often becomes paralysed with terror and crouches helplessly, waiting for the final pounce and bite through the neck. When they are desperately hungry in late winter, stoats occasionally band together in packs, probably on the move from a foodless area to find better hunting elsewhere, and at such rare times they have been known to attack humans. J. Wentworth Day, in his book *Sporting Adventure* (Harrap, 1937), told of an incident in Yorkshire on a March day, when Sir Alfred Pease, 'a brave man, and a brave man who knows more about animals than most', fought off a pack of stoats with a stick after they had leaped out at him from a hedge. Sir Alfred was a hunter of lions and a famous shot, but he ran for his life from those little devils.

A gentler excitement and one you are (mercifully) more likely to experience on a hedgerow walk is the sight of a fox creeping quietly along in search of rabbits or mice. Foxes also eat slugs, beetles, worms, young birds and eggs – almost every form of wildlife a hedge can provide. If you freeze into absolute stillness the moment you spot a fox, it may give you a few moments to admire the glowing redness of its coat and the delicate way it picks up its black-stockinged feet. Downwind of a fox you will get a whiff of the rank smell that terrifies a rabbit into the same kind of helplessness that a stoat induces. Upwind, your own smell will send the fox bounding off into safety on the far side of the hedge – a sight that never fails to thrill.

All this richness of tree, flower, bird and animal life of the hedgerow has been greatly diminished in recent years as farmers have ripped out hedges to accommodate the ever-increasing size and ever-decreasing manoeuvrability of their farm machinery. For a time in the 1960s, hedges were being removed in the Midlands and the South of England at the rate of more than a yard per acre per year – perhaps 5,000 miles (8,000km) of hedgerow in one year, many of these hedges several hundred years old and the refuge of a complex, balanced and interdependent wildlife community that had developed gradually over the centuries. A few hours with a mechanical digger is all that it takes to destroy such a priceless asset of the countryside. Many farmers, having asked themselves where all the birds and flowers they once enjoyed have gone and why the good topsoil of their enormous prairie fields is being blown away by the wind, have realised the answer and stopped ripping out their hedges. Some, such as the Berrys of Billingsmoor Farm in Devon (mentioned in Chapter 3), have set themselves the task of planting new hedges, although it will take centuries more of slow development to replace what has been lost. In Northern Ireland, where farming tends to be smaller-scale and less mechanised than in mainland Britain, there is still a good network of hedges, along which the crimson 'Chinese lanterns' of fuchsia make a brave and characteristic show. But in many areas of Britain – for example, East Anglia with its fertile soil which is so suitable for grain – the hedges continue to disappear. No one who has wandered along the hedgerows could doubt the richness and variety of the wildlife they shelter; they are a natural treasure-chest whose plundering has to stop, sooner rather than later.

WOODLAND

Woodland Visitor Centre, Monteviot, Jedburgh, Borders, Scotland.
Interpretation Centre: use of woodlands and timber. Exhibitions; woodland walks; pinery.

Although nothing survives of the wildwood that covered Britain from about 7,500BC, much of Britain's deciduous woodland (that is, woods made up largely of trees that shed their leaves in autumn) is descended from that primeval forest. Some of Britain's woodlands have been growing in the same place since at least early medieval times. They have been cut and cut again, and have naturally regenerated. They have been managed and exploited by man throughout the centuries, and used for firewood, building materials, tools, animal grazing and just about every function imaginable.

The development of artificial materials has greatly reduced the dependence of man on the trees that grow in the countryside, but how impoverished the appearance of the landscape, and how thin its wildlife, would be without them. A hillside of oak, a hanger of beech lining the edge of a downland escarpment, a wood of ash trees spread along a clifftop – these give the surrounding fields, ridges and hollows their shape and dignity. Woodlands bring an ever-changing freshness to the most familiar of views across country as they shift colour and density with infinite subtlety from the black bareness of winter to the tender green of spring, the dark, hard greenness of summer and the autumn reds and browns. To walk for hours among the old beeches and oaks of Savernake Forest in Wiltshire, for example, or under the hornbeams of Epping Forest or among the ancient coppiced oaks of the Wyre Forest in Worcestershire is a treat in itself, but for me woodland rambling is at its best when it forms a series of interludes in a walk in the open country. The pleasure comes not just from stepping into shade and leafy quiet from a sunny field, or from ducking under a sheltering canopy of leaves from pelting rain in the open. There is also the fascination of seeing evidence of the many ways the wood has been used by man down the years, and the contrast in the wildlife of the wood and its surrounding countryside.

Coppicing is the chief method of extracting shoots and other usable wood without destroying the trees. Oak, hazel, ash and chestnut are the trees most likely to be coppiced, to form what is known as 'underwood'. The stem is cut off close to the ground and the long poles put out by the cut trunk are harvested every five to fifteen years. Traditionally, the poles were used mostly for firewood, although they were also used for fencing, tool handles and the intertwined shoots that were packed with clay to make wattle-and-daub walls for medieval house-building. The fully grown trees, or 'standards', that tower over the sawn-off boles of coppiced trees in such woods look as if they must be far older, but they are probably only a hundred or so years old at most, left standing to provide shelter for the coppice until they are ready to be cut down for timber. The coppiced stumps, on the other hand, that regrow their shoots for harvesting every few years, may have survived for many centuries. The boles of some coppiced ash trees can measure up to 20ft (6m) across and could be as much as a thousand years old.

Another way of harvesting wood repeatedly is by pollarding the tree – that is, cutting it at the top of the trunk where the branches begin to spread, far enough from the ground to prevent animals eating the young shoots as soon as they appear. Willows are often pollarded; the tree has a tendency to put out such tall and heavy branches from its short base that they weigh down on and split the trunk unless the willow is pollarded. An excellent example of old willows that have grown wild and split apart can be seen along the River Misbourne, near Chalfont St Giles in Buckinghamshire. Pollarding was often carried out on the trees of wood pasture, where the land had the dual use of tree growing and animal grazing. Not only did the pollarding prevent the pigs, cows and sheep from nibbling off new shoots, but it also prevented the trees from thickening and casting too much shade for the pasture under them to thrive.

The great age of some of these coppiced or pollarded woods can be identified by several features. They often have earth banks around their perimeters, some with an old hedge on top, many with a ditch on the outer edge as added security against incursion by animals. Ancient woods tend to have a wavering, in-and-out shape around the perimeter, caused, like the snaking shape of a very old hedge, by the changing ownership and the use of the wood itself and its neighbouring fields. You may find a bowl-shaped depression among the trees, which is the dried bed of an old pond, in a landscape whose field ponds have long since been ploughed into invisibility; or the line of a centuries-old trackway or field wall which runs intact through the trees until it flattens and vanishes abruptly as it meets the ploughlands outside.

Glenariff Forest Park and Nature Reserve, Glens of Antrim, Co Antrim. Information (026 673) 232. Valley walks beside river and waterfalls in unsmartened woodland; Visitor Centre; restaurant and shop.

Stott Park Bobbin Mill, Finsthwaite, Lake Windermere, Cumbria. 1835 belt-driven bobbin mill. Coppicing of poles for manufacture of lathe-turned wooden bobbins, cotton reels, toggles, etc.

Bailey Einon Wood, near Llandrindod Wells, Powys, Mid-Wales. Oak and ash woodland, managed by the Herefordshire and Radnorshire Nature Trust. Hazel coppiced on 15-year rotation. Birds include pied flycatcher, redstart, green and greater spotted woodpecker, nuthatch, willow warbler. Purple hairstreak and speckled wood butterflies.

Coverts are stands of trees, usually small, that were either planted, or left behind after a big area of woodland was felled, to provide cover for game. Allowed to grow as thick and as tangled as nature permits, their dense undergrowth gives deep shelter and refuge to pheasants, woodcock, foxes and other creatures. On the other hand, the shooting enthusiast or huntsman knows exactly where he is likely to find his intended victims. Many long thin belts of trees were planted in the eighteenth and nineteenth centuries for the same purpose, or to provide shelter for roads and tracks that ran along exposed ridges.

Other deciduous woodlands of the British landscape are the parks that were planted by landlords in times past to provide timber and wild game, and to beautify their broad acres. Here the familiar oak, ash and beech may be interspersed with exotic pines or foreign broadleaved trees that were introduced by the Georgian or Victorian landlord when his new wood was being planted. Nineteenth-century landowners were often great amateur sylviculturalists, introducing evergreen species such as Douglas fir, Norway spruce, Corsican pine and Japanese larch – trees that are now grown commercially by the Forestry Commission. Parkland woods were planted by nobles and gentry, by bishops and abbots, as well as by the king. Their outlines tend to be more regular, whether angular or circular, than the ancient natural woodlands, and the perimeter ditch may be found inside the encircling bank rather than outside, to prevent the woodland game animals from escaping.

The broadleaved woodlands contain trees of many and varied types, but most are based on the 'big three' among British hardwoods – oak, ash and beech. Oak woods grow all over Britain. Stouthearted, strong and enduring, the oak is the quintessential British tree. It can take up to two centuries to mature, and can grow well over 100ft (30m) tall and develop a trunk 30ft (9m) or more around. There are two main types of oak: the common or pedunculate oak, which is found mostly in the South and East, and the sessile oak, which is more common the further north and west you travel. The two types are not difficult to tell apart: common oak has leaves that are joined to the twig with hardly any stem and acorns on a long stalk; sessile oak has long-stemmed leaves and short-stalked acorns. In parkland woods, or in woods grown for their attractiveness in a landowner's eyes, you may also discover the evergreen holm oak or ilex, with dark green, leathery leaves and bark that is cracked into small plates like the skin of a crocodile.

Oaks harbour a variety of galls, which are swellings grown by the tree around the grubs of gall wasps. Some take the form of marble galls – hard brown balls which grow where the grub is encased in a shoot; others are oak apples (soft pink blobs) and spangle galls (red scabs) which both develop on the leaves.

In the days of sail oak timber was used for shipbuilding because of its great strength. It also had many other functions where sturdiness was the main requirement – beams, lintels and frames of

Westonbirt Arboretum, near Tetbury, Gloucestershire. Well over 150 acres (61ha) of trees, started in 1829. Native and foreign species include pines, cypresses, firs; oaks, limes, hornbeams, whitebeams, beeches, poplars, maples, hickories. Many rare exotic species include Japanese horse-chestnut, ebony, wing-nut, small-leaved ash. Rhododendron collection.

houses, spokes of wooden wheels and strong large items of furniture.

Hedgerow oaks seldom have the opportunity to grow to their full height nowadays because the mechanical hedge-slasher cuts them off regardless, at the height of the rest of the hedge.

> Oak before ash,
> We're in for a splash –
> Ash before oak,
> We're in for a soak

goes the old rhyme. Ash and oak are often found growing together, the ash putting out its long, toothed leaves up to a month after the oak unless a wet summer is in prospect. The drip from ash leaves is poisonous to almost all plants, resulting in a patch of earth under the tree that is bare of undergrowth. Ash wood burns hot, shapes well and is hard. In the past its main use was for firewood, and for making gates, wheel rims and tool handles which needed to withstand repeated blows and hammerings.

Beech trees, with their smooth grey trunks and oval pointed leaves, are found wherever there is chalk, and in many other areas of limestone or loam in the south of England especially. Beech woods on the escarpment of chalk downland are known as 'hangers'. They were often planted for miles along ridgetop roads to break the force of wind and rain with their great spreading branches and thick foliage. Like the ash, their leaf drip poisons most undergrowth, often leaving the tree standing in a circle of bare ground. Beech timber is light and white, splitting and bending to make superb, pale-coloured furniture. For all the brightness of its wood, however, the beech in my estimation is a cold tree. A ramble in an autumn or winter beech wood feels several degrees colder than a walk among other types of trees. Oak woods generally hold an atmosphere of serenity and warmth, ash woods of lightness and gaiety. But a walk through a beech wood feels solemn and mysterious – sometimes a shivery experience, or even a menacing one.

Of course, the broadleaved woodlands contain many tree species other than oak, ash and beech – the sycamore, for example, and the sweet chestnut, the poplar and the hornbeam, and the lime with its round leaves of lovely translucent green. Take a pocket tree identification book with you on your woodland rambles – you won't begrudge the extra weight.

A flower book is a good companion on a woodland walk, for woods shelter a wide variety of plants. On soils that are rich in lime, carpets of green-leaved, green-flowered dog's mercury grow under the trees. Woodruff forms thick carpets, too, its pointed leaves turning upwards to form a spiky cup under the bunch of tiny white flowers that sprout from the top of the stem. Larger white flowers with five petals, streaked with purple or mauve lines, are those of wood sorrel. You may be lucky enough to find a bird's-nest orchid in the

A belt of trees planted to shelter an exposed road.

Richly coloured bracken glows under Welsh oak woodland.

shady parts of beech woods, a ghostly looking plant with pale brown, fragile flowers that seems at first glance to be withered and dead. In woods on neutral soils – that is, neither lime-laden nor acid – grow early purple orchids with dark purple flowers, sheets of bluebells, clumps of primroses and the big six-petalled white flowers of wood anemone. Acid soils may offer you lesser stitchwort, whose five white petals are split almost to the base, and the round green leaves and round white stem-clasping flowers of wintergreen (which is often also found in coniferous woods).

The bird life of broadleaved woods is as rich and varied as their plant populations. Among the larger birds are pheasants that cry 'cok-cok' and explode from under your feet with enough clatter to make you jump; crows on the prowl for nestlings and eggs; sparrowhawks sitting in a tree ready to swoop on to a victim, then swerving between the trunks to grab a small bird in mid-flight; buzzards mewing above the trees; green woodpeckers with their ringing call like hysterical laughter and their dipping flight; jays cackling and swearing at you, the woodland's early warning system, before flitting off with a flash of blue from their wing feathers.

Smaller birds include the chiff-chaff, whose endless two-note repetition of its name ticks and tocks through the trees; the tree-creeper sometimes seen crawling up a tree trunk looking for insects to pick out of the bark with its curved beak; the slaty-blue, buff-bellied nuthatch which wedges a nut into the bark and axes it open with its bill; and the long-tailed tit, which is distinguishable from the other tits by its pink belly and its tail as long as the rest of its body.

The woodland has become the stronghold of the badger, whose home, or 'sett', is dug out among the tree roots or in the bank on the outskirts of the wood to form a wonderful subterranean tangle of tunnels, sleeping chambers, entrances and exits. The badger is a clean and tidy-minded householder who digs special latrine pits and ejects its old bedding. This dried-up 'rake' found near the entrance holes to a sett is a sure sign that badgers are in occupation. Other clues are coarse white or black hairs caught in tree bark a few feet from the ground, trunks rubbed smooth at the same height in their role as scratching posts and freshly dug earth around the sett marked with the print of a five-toed pad.

You will have to come back to the wood at nightfall or in the early dawn and sit still for a long time to catch a sight of the animal itself, as badgers are nocturnal and do almost all of their above-ground business by night. They eat just about everything that comes their way – carrion or dead animals, fruits, berries, wasp grubs, beetles, slugs, young rabbits, worms. They do not hibernate in the winter, although activity may slow down. They have evolved an effective method of producing their young at the right time of year when food is abundant – the female, after a spring mating, can carry the fertilised eggs within her for nine months until the following December before they are finally implanted in her uterus and start to develop. The young badgers, which are born in February, the hardest time of winter, are weaned and active enough to find their own food just as spring arrives and food is available for them.

No positive proof has been found of the badger's alleged role as a carrier of bovine tuberculosis, but the suspicions of farmers have been awakened and many now think of the badger as a pest that must be exterminated. There are those who are only too keen to help farmers – the gangs who come to the sett at night to dig out the badgers by torchlight and enjoy the 'sport' of holding them down while dogs are encouraged to attack and kill them. Badger-digging was made illegal as long ago as 1878, but the thrill of getting the better of a frightened and harmless animal seems to be heightened by the added thrill of breaking the law. A bite from the formidable crushing mechanism of a badger's jaws is a nasty prospect. One can only hope that the persecuted animals occasionally manage to get their teeth into a badger-baiter's hand. If anyone other than the badger suffers, though, it is probably the equally blameless and victimised dogs that do the baiter's dirty work for him.

In a thick carpet of leaves in winter you may find the rolled prickly ball of a hibernating hedgehog, with all its systems shut down until the spring. Grey squirrels leap from branch to branch or scuttle along the ground trailing their long tails like a plume of smoke. Once on a tree trunk they will whip around to the far side; look 10 feet higher and you may well spot a beady black eye peeping around the edge of the trunk or a branch, keeping you under observation. The red squirrels that once colonised all the British woodlands have been driven out almost to extinction since their grey cousins were introduced from North America, but in Scottish woods you can often get a glimpse of their fox-red coats against the birch or pine trunks.

The coniferous woodland of Britain has its own variety of wildlife, which makes up for the often regimented walks down criss-cross, dead straight rides and footpaths which are planned and kept clear by the Forestry Commission. Personally, I like to walk in coniferous forests, for the resinous smell of the pine trees and the sighing of the wind in their branches; but some people find it boring or sinister – all those millions of trees, all just the same. Since the establishment of the Forestry Commission in 1919 to make Britain self-sufficient in timber, many hundreds of thousands of acres of otherwise marginal land, most of it sandy or acid, have been planted with conifers, as described in Chapter 1. The plan is to plant to the point where, by the year 2000, about 10 per cent of Britain's land area will be under woodland of one sort or another – about 5 million acres (2 million ha), of which three-fifths will be new forests.

Certain types of trees are likely to be noticed on a walk in coniferous woodland. Douglas fir was introduced to Britain in about 1828, and was named after the collector for the Royal Horticultural Society, David Douglas, who sent home its seeds from Canada. Its timber grows long and straight, and as the tree can reach heights of more than 200ft (60m), it was very widely used in the days of sail to make masts and spars. The shape is distinctive – its branches point outwards and upwards towards the top, horizontally out in the middle and turn downwards towards the bottom of the tree. Grand fir, which was also introduced by David Douglas, is commonly grown by the Forestry Commission and is one of the fastest-growing conifers.

The pyramid-shaped Norway spruce, or Christmas tree, is found throughout the plantations; once a native of Britain, it disappeared with the post-Ice Age spread of the broadleaved forests and was not seen again until it was reintroduced some time in the early sixteenth century. The Norway spruce's roots delve only shallowly into the ground, so after a gale you will find uprooted specimens throughout a wood.

A cousin of the Norway spruce, the Sitka spruce has a bluish tinge to the foliage, which is hard and sharp and capable of jabbing you unpleasantly if you brush carelessly past. Spruce wood is also straight and strong, and is excellent for the big timber jobs such as the roof trusses of new houses.

Lake Vyrnwy, near Llanfyllin, Clwyd, North Wales. Coniferous woodland around the lake attracts many kinds of birds, including siskin, crossbill, sparrowhawk and black grouse. Deciduous woods hold pied flycatcher, redstart and wood warbler as summer visitors. Red squirrels, polecat and badger also to be seen.

Queen Elizabeth Forest Park, Aberfoyle, Central Region, Scotland. Visitor Centre with audio-visual exhibition of Forest Park through the four seasons. Information and displays on forestry and wildlife of the area. Forest trails from centre; waymarked forest walks, cycle trails.

Farigaig Forest Centre, Inverfarigaig, Loch Ness, Highland, Scotland. Forestry Commission Interpretation Centre: conservation of forest wildlife. Forest walks from centre.

Springtime fun in the bluebell woods.

The bushy Corsican pine and the Scots and Lodgepole pines are widely grown for their immensely useful timber, of which every grade is used for everything from paper pulp to fencing, industrial palettes and construction timber.

Of all the commercially grown conifers the larch is my favourite. It is a really graceful and delicate tree with feathery, soft leaves on branches that sweep down to upturned tips, giving the whole tree balance and symmetry, and at the same time a soft outline. The larch is the only conifer to shed its leaves in winter. Autumn walks in larch woods are beautifully coloured, as the larch leaves (which are light green in the European larch and greeny-blue in the Japanese larch) turn brilliant gold and then red before falling.

Among coniferous trees with their smoky, heavy silence and dark shade, two small birds in particular make welcome little splashes and spurts of colour and noise – the coal tit and the goldcrest, which are so often seen in each other's company that the rambler instinctively looks and listens for one on spotting the other. The coal tit's pale belly shows up well on a pine twig overhead, as does the little white cap on the back of its black head. Its song is squeaky, piping and complaining. The goldcrest sings even higher, a diminutive saw-like 'zee-zee' that is repeated over and over again by this tiny greenish-brown bird with the bold orange streak down the middle of its black cap.

In Scottish coniferous woodland you may hear a flurry among the blaeberries and heather and see the turkey-sized capercaillie lurching away with its tail spread like a big fan, in a bounding flight a few feet above the ground. Capercaillies were reintroduced into Scotland in early Victorian times after having been exterminated by shooting and by clearance of the pine forests where they lived. Their most endearing feature, after that startled-dowager flight, is the bold scarlet stripe on their upper eye skin. The male's mating song is said to be something worth hearing. It has three movements – the first a noise like someone trying to be sick, the second like a champagne cork being pulled and the third like a knife being very softly whetted against a rough stone. Female capercaillies, though, think it is a wonderful sound.

The grey squirrel, usurper of the woods from the native red squirrel.

HEATHS

Heaths, because they are sandy and dry, have been under tremendous pressure from housing development. Some heaths in Dorset, for example, have been almost completely destroyed. While, historically, heaths gave decent rough grazing, they were always far enough down the agricultural ladder to be vulnerable to enclosure and attempts at reclamation for crops or pasture. But a good part of the New Forest is still heathland, as is much of the Breckland country around Thetford on the Norfolk/Suffolk border, and here one can wander the trails through heather and bilberry.

Gorse and broom are two very characteristic heath plants, the prickly gorse bushes with buttery-yellow flowers smelling deliciously of coconut when the sun warms them. Broom has yellow flowers, too, but no prickles. Its long whip-like spikes of leaves sprout black seed-pods which you can hear cracking and snapping as the warmth of the sunshine causes them to split and shoot their seeds over a wide area. The low purple flowerheads of wild thyme grow bushily on mats of dark green leaves that give out that tongue-tingling thyme smell when they are crushed or bruised. Common cudweed is another typical plant of heathland, its tightly packed heads of tiny white flowers sprouting long yellow fringes that make the whole flowerhead look yellow, its stem silvered with soft hairs. The delicate, pale blue harebell does well on heaths, and in wet parts you may come across the sundew, in whose sticky red hairs its insect victims lie, being dissolved into sundew food.

Wheatears frequent stony heaths as they do the limestone uplands and moors, and in brambly thickets you may hear the sweet song of a whitethroat, or see it bobbing vertically up and down while it sings, as if it is dangling on elastic. The bird has a pink-brown breast and a white chin-strap. Another heathland bird is the grasshopper warbler, which is also fond of hiding in the bushier places; you are less likely to see it than to hear its monotonous clicking song like a rusty old fishing reel being wound.

Heathlands are some of the last strongholds of the nightjar, whose numbers have been decreasing in direct proportion to the disappearance of the heaths themselves. You will be lucky indeed to spot a nightjar in the daytime when it lies camouflaged among the twigs of its scraped nest, its plumage being the same grey and brown speckled colour. But in the evening or at night you may hear its hunting cry 'coo-ic' (which is not as sharp as the tawny owl's 'kee-wick!') as it flies after moths, using its beard of fine bristles as a radar receiver for nearby aerial movement. Country people once believed that its big mouth, which is necessary for gobbling moths on the wing, was used for sucking milk from the teats of goats as they lay sleeping – hence its nickname of 'goatsucker'.

Heaths are not good places to do your summer walking in shorts and sockless sandals; as well as the sharp gravelly stones and gorse prickles, there may be adders basking on the sand and stones in the sunshine. Common and green lizards like these hot dry places too, as do horseflies that can give a sharp, painful bite as a reminder that you should cover your legs next time. A pleasanter flying inhabitant of the heath is the green hairstreak butterfly, whose green caterpillar feeds on bramble, gorse and bird's-foot trefoil. The adult butterfly's top wing surfaces are dull brown, but on the underside when the wings are folded you can spot a hair-like streak of white on the drab green background of the hind-wing.

WETLANDS

If scarcity of water is one of the features of heathland, superabundance of moisture is the keynote of wetland. In these flat places it is water, or man's attempt to control its influence, that moulds and dominates the landscape. Wetlands have their own specialised wildlife communities – and their own hazards and difficulties, if you are thinking of taking a walk to see that wildlife. Their fields or patches of grazing tend to be squared off and separated by water-filled drainage ditches. The footpaths, by another ramification of Sod's Law, usually take you around three and a half sides of a field before you find that the plank footbridge across the ditch has snapped in two and sunk in the mire. They are places where you will find yourself floundering, wet to the knees, stranded and forced to backtrack. Many ramblers think that the awkwardness of this landscape and its refusal to come an inch to meet the visitor is a great part of its charm. Wetlands – whether in the East Anglian fens, the Somerset Levels, the west coast of Wales, the Scottish lowlands or the 'slobs' of Northern Ireland – are uncompromising places, damp marshy sponges where rivers overflow and the water table is just below or at the surface level, if it is not well above it.

Based as most of them are on underlying areas of fertile moss peat or alluvial soil, wetlands are vulnerable to ploughing. Many succumbed in the 1970s, when Common Market incentives to farmers to produce more and more food were at their peak. Conservationists made a fuss each time that the slowly evolved and delicately maintained balance of wildlife was ripped out in the space of a day or so. Some farmers responded by staying their hands. Many did not. One man in Norfolk ploughed a great V-sign to 'busy-bodies' in the middle of a patch of marsh that local naturalists had been trying to persuade him to reprieve.

Being natural sponges that soak up run-off water from the surrounding farmland, the wetland ground and watercourses are very prone to poisoning from agricultural chemicals. Flooding is a problem, but not as much as you might suppose. Plants and animals adapt surprisingly well (and far better than humans in the same circumstances), some leading a semi-amphibious life that allows them to survive in almost all wetland conditions. Some wetlands, like the great marsh of Mòine Mhór, near Loch Crinan on Scotland's west coast, are scarcely under drainage at all. Others, like the marshes of agricultural east Norfolk or the Somerset Levels, are controlled by

Cambridge and County Folk Museum, 2–3 Castle Street, Cambridge. Housed in sixteenth-century former White Horse Inn. Traditional tools used by fenmen for digging drainage dykes and harvesting peat. Also former inn bar, cooking and lighting exhibits, Victorian kitchen, domestic crafts (including lace-making and embroidery), city and university display and children's room.

Wicken Fen Nature Reserve, Wicken, near Soham, Cambridgeshire. Oldest nature reserve in the country: 600 acres (242ha) of undrained, unimproved fen. Sanctuary for many birds, insects, plants and animals. Information centre with displays. Bird-viewing hides.

The Willows Peat Company, Shapwick Road, Westhay, near Glastonbury, Somerset. Peat Moors Visitor Centre: displays on wildlife of Somerset Levels wetlands.

Love is never out of style while the gorse is in bloom.

sluices, ditches, gates, pumps and endless human endeavour to keep the water in its place and the land in good fettle. All are highly individual places and all are brimful of fresh and stagnant water.

In wetlands such as the Fens, where water running from the hills brings plenty of lime with it, you may find marsh bedstraw, a straggling plant with a thin stem from which clusters of tiny white flowers shoot off at odd angles and bunches of short leaves hang down at intervals like the fringe on an Edwardian lampshade. Other tiny flowers are the pale pink ones of marsh valerian and the white of milk parsley which sprout in a bunch from the top of a thick green or purple stem. Large conspicuous flowers belong to the greater spearwort (yellow) and arrowhead (white and three-petalled, with a dark purple spot in the middle). Arrowhead, which grows in shallow water, gets its name from its big leaves, which are pointed and barbed like the business end of an arrow. Marsh helleborine is another wetland plant with conspicuous flowers – white inside and pink outside at the base, with crinkled edges – that hang out from the stem like a tower of bells.

In marshy ground that is neither lime-soaked nor acid grow the massed ranks of yellow iris with long rushy leaves and big drooping

yellow flowers; also the sweet-smelling meadowsweet whose little white flowers froth around the red stem in bubbly heads. In the ditches and watercourses grow pondweed and the great white saucers of water-lilies, while in the boggy margins are bright yellow marsh marigolds.

On the acid peat wetlands where the ground is sodden into bogs, plants that are often seen on a squelchy ramble are bogbean, its three-lobed leaves appearing above water level and its pink and white petals tufted with a soft fuzz; the six sharp-pointed orange petals of bog asphodel; the insect-catching common sundew, with tiny white flowers on the graceful curve of the stem and round red leaves covered in sticky hairs to trap its prey; and marsh pennywort, with pink flowers so small that you may overlook them altogether and round discs of leaves.

Wetland trees tend not to grow as tall as those of drier, higher country; one that does is the aspen, which can reach 50ft (15m) and more. Aspen bark is smooth and greyish and its rounded leaves with their jagged edges tremble and whisper in every slight breeze at the ends of long thin stalks. There is nothing quite as conducive to drifting off into sleep as lying on a warm day in the shade of a

Pollarded willows lean over a rhyne in the Somerset Levels.

Broadland Conservation Centre, Ranworth Broad, Norwich, Norfolk. Thatched, floating Information Centre moored at end of Ranworth Broad Nature Trail. Exhibition of natural history of the Norfolk Broads, man's influence on them and their conservation. Viewing gallery with binoculars, overlooking Ranworth Broad. Duckboard nature trail through the various stages by which a broad reverts from open water to mature woodland.

Broads Museum, Sutton Windmill, near Stalham, Norfolk. Housed in restored 1789 windmill, the tallest in Britain. Museum covers many aspects of traditional life and work in the Norfolk Broads and their wildlife.

grove of aspens, listening to the dreamy rushing whisper of their leaves.

Alder is another round-leaved tree which grows in groves by the waters of wetlands, and willows will thrive anywhere in damp conditions. In the Norfolk Broads, where the traditional management of these old flooded peat diggings by cutting their reeds and sedges for thatch has all but ceased, the open water of many broads has reverted through a stage of reed and sedge fen to carr woodland, where alder and willow form dense thickets with their feet in or near the water. On the Somerset Levels the willow shoots – or withies, as they are locally known – are harvested to be stripped of their bark, dried and woven into baskets. They make excellent eel and salmon traps that will last a whole season in the water, but these days such items are rarely seen in use.

What kinds of butterflies you may see in the wetlands depends mainly on two factors: whether their main foodplants grow where you are walking and how many people go walking there as well. The wilder and less frequented the location, the more you are likely to have your walk graced by the sight of butterflies darting over water and marsh. A few of the more unusual and therefore exciting possibilities are suggested here. By far the most spectacular is the black and yellow swallowtail, with its two red spots near the twin points of the tail; the largest butterfly resident in Britain, it feeds chiefly on milk parsley. You will have to go to the Norfolk Broads to see the swallowtail, although efforts are currently being made to reintroduce it to the Wicken Fen nature reserve in Cambridgeshire.

In grass marshland in the extreme west of Britain – western Scotland, the upper portion of north-west England, west Wales and the West Country – where the bushy round blue flowerheads of devil's-bit scabious grow, a sighting of the marsh fritillary is an occasional treat. Its wings are patched with squares of warm orange and pale yellow with white dots in a curved line around the trailing edges of the hind-wings.

Another butterfly that is confined to a few locations in Britain – in this case the mountains of the Lake District and central Scotland, above 1,500ft (457m) – is the small mountain ringlet, whose dark wings have a band of red arches with black central dots. Bright sunlight brings out this butterfly to feed on the flowers of mat grass.

A fellow frequenter of the peat bogs of north Wales, northern England, Ireland and Scotland is the orange-brown large heath butterfly, with dark spots surrounded by white circles on the undersides of its wings. Beaked rush is its foodplant.

In the East Anglian fens, with a slice of luck you may set eyes on the large copper's brilliant orange, dark-edged wings – it is a reintroduction, having been wiped out a century ago by heedless collectors and by the drainage of most of the fens it inhabited.

Wherever watercourses thread the wetlands you are more than likely to see a heron standing stock still at the water's edge, waiting its chance to step forward with lowered head and stab a passing fish or eel with its sword-like bill. After striking, the heron will often drop its prey on the bank and watch its last writhings, impassively, before demolishing it with quick pecks and swallows. There may be several voles, frogs and small fish in the heron's craw by the time it takes off and lumbers into the air with great slow flaps of its ragged wings. In flight it sails massively along, beating the air heavily, its head and neck tucked well back and legs trailing out behind, its feet neatly together.

A large hawk seen from time to time over the East Anglian marshes is the marsh harrier, which flaps slowly low over the reed-beds looking for frogs, water voles and young moorhens and other birds. Its wing-tips spread in a 'hand' of outstretched feathers like those of an eagle. The best place for a likely sighting is the RSPB reserve at Minsmere, on the Suffolk coast near Dunwich, where marsh harriers thrive.

Snipe flash low over marshy ground, zig-zagging away from intrusive humans to make a hard-to-hit target.

A big bird which is rarely seen, but occasionally heard giving out its famous echoing boom from the reed-beds, is the bittern, which, when alarmed, stretches its head and neck up vertically to blend in with the reeds. The bittern was extinct in the Fenlands by 1850, but it made a cautious return in the early years of this century and has slowly increased its numbers and range.

Reed-beds provide good camouflage and nesting sites for the reed warbler, which has a brown back and pale coffee-coloured breast. You will see it grasping a reed stem with both feet, then jumping to another like an acrobat. The reed warbler weaves its nest into a solid cup, supported by the scaffolding of several reed stems. Its song stutters along with little bursts of repetition: 'pic, pic, pic . . . pirrip! pirrip!'

A much more colourful and noticeable reed-bed inhabitant is the bearded tit, although you need to choose a remote and undisturbed spot to see it. Although it is shaped like a tit, the bird is, in fact, a cousin of the thrush, its proper name being the bearded reedling. It whirrs over the reeds, showing a fine pair of black moustaches, a golden-red back and a long tit-like tail.

The reed bunting nests and feeds in all kinds of thick low vegetation near water in wetland areas. The female is as drab as a sparrow, but the male has a smart white collar under a black head. It flits among the reeds in jerky swoops and flicks its tail when perching.

The South American coypu, which is the size of a large dog with a blunt beaver-like face, colonised many of the East Anglian wetlands for a time after some had escaped from experimental coypu farms. Although they are so large, the coypus survived until the late 1980s and could often be seen swimming across fenland streams and be heard crashing through the reed-beds. But they did a considerable amount of damage with their bank-burrowing and gnawing of crops, so war was declared and a price was put on their heads. After a great deal of indiscriminate shooting by farmers, Ministry marksmen and

In the margins between land and water grow the bright yellow marsh marigolds.

(Below) A rich tangle of waterlogged carr woodland.

(Opposite) Reeds grow tall around Hickling Broad in Norfolk.

trappers wiped out the entire population of coypus. However, it would be nice to think that somewhere in the fens the last of the coypus is holding out and preparing a comeback, like Hereward the Wake.

The otter has also been on the point of extinction, having been hunted with dogs, shot by farmers and harried wherever it showed itself. The cause of this slaughter seems to have been just as much pure tradition as the desire to safeguard fish stocks. Now otter hunting and shooting have virtually stopped; they would have been forced to come to an end, anyway, as the otter is no longer to be found along most British rivers.

Parts of the Scottish and Irish Highland and island coasts are hosts to sea otters, but to see the otter of freshwater habitats you will probably have your best chance in the wetlands. If you are not lucky enough to see the animal itself with its webbed feet and long thick 'rudder', or tail, swimming along the bottom of a watercourse followed by a string of bubbles or slipping down the bank into the water, look for its spraints, or droppings, on a rock by or in the water – the spraints are tarry black and full of fish bones and scales.

It is ironical that the British otter population may have been saved from being hunted to extinction, only to be endangered again by pollution and over-use of the countryside. Otters are susceptible to poisoning by all kinds of agricultural and industrial water pollution, through the fish, frogs and waterside invertebrates they eat, and from the water itself in which they spend most of their time. Properly wary of human presence, they were never equipped by nature to deal with the stresses and dangers of being a twentieth-century water animal. Only the dedicated work of such places as the Otter Trust at Earsham in Suffolk gives any hope for the future of this beautiful and characterful animal.

RIVERS, PONDS, LAKES AND RESERVOIRS

Water is the most popular feature of any country ramble, whether in the form of river, pond, lake or reservoir. The flow of a river seems to carry you effortlessly on for mile upon mile, while the shape of a lake is an invitation to make a round walk. Besides the usual plants, flowers and birds there are others that you only find close to the water or in it. Rivers in their length penetrate many different kinds of countryside and built-up areas, too, and bring these influences – some good, some bad – along with them. You never know just how the water will be. Yesterday's scummy ooze and today's sparklingly clear flow may be tomorrow's charging brown torrent. Rivers become ever more precious as sources and refuges of wildlife in the landscape, while they are vulnerable themselves to pollution from farm and factory.

Plants of the river valleys and flood plains do particularly well in the rich alluvial soils of those areas. Many are the same as those that are found in the wetlands – after all, rivers and still water are the wetlands' main feature. Some others are outlined here. On the

The Otter Trust, Earsham, near Bungay, Suffolk. Largest collection of otters in the world. Mobile Exhibition Centre (sometimes out on tour), with display explaining importance of wetlands and the otter's place in them. Otters in pens of graded size and wildness to ready them for release into their natural habitat.

Vane Farm Nature Centre, near Kinross, Loch Leven, Tayside, Scotland. Converted farm buildings with displays on loch and countryside. Binoculars, observation hide, nature trail. Huge numbers of ducks and geese on Loch Leven, especially in winter.

river banks comfrey glows white or purple, its bell-shaped flowers growing on a curling stem that forms a whorl. Himalayan balsam is found in great pinky-purple drifts all along river banks, anywhere where it has the area to itself. A tall plant on a thick red stem, its petals make a pair of full, open lips, exposing a spotted throat. Like broom, Himalayan balsam fires its seeds from capsules with an audible snap if you brush against them. It was introduced from India in 1839, but as a garden escape has thrived in a remarkable way in Britain's very different climate. Another tall plant is the hairy-stemmed and pink-flowered great willowherb, whose seeds travel not by pop-gun fire but by parachute, floating off for miles under their tufts of silky hairs. Hemp agrimony likes river banks, its tall red stem carrying a thick bunch of straggly, furry-looking small flowers of a rich, deep pink; and near the water grow the bushy, lilac-pink flowerheads of water mint, which is soft and hairy to touch.

At the edge of the running water are the little bright blue flowers of brooklime, their stalks sprouting from below the topmost leaves of the stem. Creeping yellow cress grows just at the margin as well, its tiny yellow flowers budding on a straggling, creeping stem with spiky leaves.

Plants that cool their toes in the water, so to speak, include the peppery-tasting leaves of watercress; rushes; the bulrush with its velvety sausage of minuscule brown flowers; greater water-parsnip, an umbellifer on a thick stem like angelica; and horsetails – green plants in jointed sections like bamboo – which are direct and almost unchanged descendants of tropical plants that grew in Britain 350 million years ago and which have been found in coal measures.

In ponds and other places of still water, some of the characteristic river plants grow. Others may include the white and yellow water-lily; the big oval leaves of broadleaved pondweed that float on the surface, and the white five-petalled flower of common water crowfoot, which has five-fingered, jagged edged leaves that float on the water and feathery leaves that trail under the surface. Duckweed grows in those familiar mats of tiny bright green leaves, two or three to each head, trailing a hair-like root below the surface. It clings to your finger if you dip it in a mass of duckweed, and to the heads and faces of cartoon characters who have fallen in the duckpond. Frogbit is another very common floating pond plant; it is a darker green than duckweed and has kidney-shaped leaves.

Where the river flows, the heron fishes. Much more rarely seen, and consequently a greater thrill when it is spotted, is the searing shot-silk blue of the kingfisher, like a line of liquid streaked in mid-air as it darts along the river. With patience and luck – and immobility – you may enjoy the sight of the kingfisher sitting on branch or bridge rail to knock a caught fish into submission before swallowing it head-first.

Dippers with their white bibs bob and bow on stones in the

Sussex Farm Museum Trust, Horam Manor Farm, Heathfield, East Sussex. Horam Quiet Corner nature trail (detailed booklet guide), leading beside several ponds, some the flooded excavations of iron ore mining. Birds, fish, water plants.

middle of shallow rivers. They can walk upstream into the flow, pressed down against the river bed by the force of the current, to hunt for minnows, worms, water beetles and dragonfly larvae.

Wagtails are very often seen by the water in their three manifestations: the black-and-white pied wagtail; the grey wagtail which, confusingly, has bright yellow underparts that are far more noticeable than its grey back, and the yellow wagtail, which really *is* mostly yellow, except for a greeny-brown back. Wagtails are always on the move, pattering forward, stopping to flick and flirt their long tails and nod their heads, then running on again – like fussy time-and-motion men keeping tabs on a production line.

In the reeds you will see moorhens with their red noses and coots with their 'bald' white brows, paddling deeper into cover, perhaps followed by a string of chicks. If the female is frightened when you come suddenly upon her, she will take off, seeming to run across the water and leaving a line of widening ripple circles behind her.

By a pond in spring you may be startled by a sudden 'smack' on the water and see a swallow flying off with a scatter of drops. Swallows skim as low as this over the water when a lowering in atmospheric pressure forces the insects on which the swallows feed down to ground and water level. Countrymen have known for centuries that if swallows smack the water the weather will shortly change for the worse. Early spring when swallows reappear in Britain on migration, and autumn when they depart again, are, of course, seasons of unsettled weather when swallows are most likely to be seen smacking the water or skimming very low over ponds. Before bird ringing and radar tracking positively proved their tremendous migrating trek to and from Africa each year, some swallows were thought to spend the winter in Britain, hibernating in the mud at the bottom of ponds. Their sudden appearance by ponds in the spring, apparently flying out of the water itself with an explosive little 'smack!', reinforced the belief.

Big lakes attract a proportionate number of wildfowl. Lough Neagh in Northern Ireland, for example – well over 100 square miles of water – is home to 30,000 pochard and 25,000 tufted duck, as well as enormous flocks of scaup, mallard, wigeon, teal, coot and goldeneye.

Modern reservoirs may be soulless places, especially those concrete basins on the outskirts of large industrial towns without the proximity of high hills to give them drama. But on these vast sheets of still water, and on flooded quarry and gravel pits, great flocks of duck and other waterbirds congregate, enhancing any morning's ramble with a pair of binoculars. The mallard drake with its gorgeous chestnut breast and iridescent green head, the duck so sadly, drably brown, are seen everywhere, as are mute swans with their bright orange upper bills and black knob-like swelling just above.

Other ducks often seen are pochard and wigeon, both with russet-red heads; and, in winter, the shoveller. Shoveller drakes have the same iridescent green head as the male mallard, shoveller

White water lilies open to the sun.

ducks the same drab brown plumage as mallard females (although with a pale blue shoulder flash), but their great blade-shaped spoons of bills mark them out at once. Through these bills they sieve water, eating what remains behind in the shape of weed, seeds, water snails and insects.

On flooded gravel pits that are not plagued by loud motor-boats, the great crested grebe may be seen feeding and nesting. This bird was virtually wiped out in Britain in the nineteenth century when its plumage was considered perfect for decorating ladies' hats. But conservationists have helped it to re-establish itself throughout the southern part of Britain. The great crested grebe has a long red bill and a black cap to its head which ends on the back in the two stubby peaks of the crest. During courtship the male and female perform a spectacular water ballet that includes such features as shaking their heads at each other, standing upright on their tails in the water and waving a beakful of weed, puffing out their crests and dashing along with heads stretched out horizontally on the surface.

Strangford Lough, Co Down. National Trust Wildlife Scheme – huge flocks of wildfowl; bird hides; interpretation centre.

Northern Ireland Aquarium, Portaferry, Strangford Lough, Co Down. Display with many live exhibits of life in the waters of Strangford Lough. Tea room.

Gibraltar Point Nature Reserve, Skegness, Lincolnshire. Visitor Centre with displays and exhibition of wildlife of reserve: 3 miles (5km) of seashore, sand-dunes, salt-marsh and freshwater marsh and mere. Guided or lone walks from centre along paths through reserve; many plants labelled. Observation platform, bird hide.

SALT-MARSH AND ESTUARY

Some of the richest wildlife walking in Britain is in that salty, muddy, windblown zone where flat land meets sea. It can take time to get a taste for a type of landscape that in rain and wind, or under dark skies, can look both blank and threatening. Nowhere feels quite as bleakly alien as a lonely salt-marsh in a rainy February dawn. Yet the marshes in winter can offer you bird-watching, particularly of geese, that may not be found in any other environment. In summer, smelling of rich fruit-cake and sprinkled with the pink of sea-lavender and the gold of samphire, they look wonderful and show a different but equally absorbing bird life.

East Anglia is the classic marsh area, where all along the Suffolk and Norfolk coasts and up through the fenlands around the Wash you can find long stretches of salt-marsh on the seaward side of the sea walls that were built to keep out the tide. Paths run for miles along the sea-wall tops, giving you a grandstand view over the marsh – and giving the birds an equally excellent view of you. You should take frequent excursions down and out into the marsh and sit down with binoculars if you want to see and not be seen. But beware – the tide can come in unexpectedly fast in such flat areas, creeping up channels in the marsh to appear suddenly between you and the safety of the sea wall.

The chief characteristic of marshland is that the tide regularly covers it. Marshland plants, therefore, have to be able to withstand inundation and heavy doses of salt. Their leaves tend to be thick and fleshy to enable them to store fresh water, and are often hairy or scaly to help repel salt. In the driest part of the marsh, the zone furthest inland, grow the big pink five-petalled flowers and hairy stem and leaves of marshmallow, whose roots were (and perhaps still are in some districts) used to make marshmallow sweets. Sea aster's flowers are like large pale purple or white daisies, with a yellow button in the centre. Scurvy grass shows four-petalled white flowers on thick reddish stems with fleshy heart-shaped leaves. Its juice, which is full of vitamin C, was drunk (mixed with spices to neutralise its nasty taste) from medieval times until the nineteenth century to ward off scurvy. Not only sailors, but anyone with a poor vitamin-deficient diet could suffer from scurvy, in which the sufferers' feet swelled, their legs became blotched with blue, their breath stank, their gums swelled and bled, and their teeth dropped out.

Nearer the tideline, where conditions are wetter and more salty, common sea-lavender grows in thick matted clumps, its tiny lavender-pink flowers in brushy strips along the tops of the stalk-ends. Golden samphire has yellow daisy-like flowers and bright green, fleshy leaves. Seablite's little cylindrical red leaves grow in bushes. But the chief marsh plant, which holds the mud together with its mazy tangle of roots, is sea purslane, great carpets of its fat silvery-green leaves giving the marsh a grey, stippled look. Where the marsh meets the mud, reddish-green insects appear to be rooted; they are the jointed stem and plump leaves of glasswort, or marsh samphire, which can be eaten straight from the marsh, pickled or boiled and served hot with butter. The long grass-like leaves of *Zostera marina*, or eel grass, grow down here at the mud margin as well, and are the favourite food of brent geese.

To the salt-marshes, particularly where a river broadens out into a wide muddy estuary, geese come to spend the winter from their summer breeding grounds in more northern countries. At any time between October and April you may spot greylag, Britain's only native breeding goose (grey-brown back, orange bill, pink legs); whitefront (brown breast barred with black, white under tail, white 'noseband'); pinkfoot (mainly on the East Coast – grey-brown body, dark head and neck, pink legs and feet); Canada goose (black head and neck, white 'chin-strap'; resident all year round since its eighteenth-century introduction as an ornamental bird). Dark-bellied brent geese, which are small and sociable, over-winter on the East Coast. At night they fly out to roost on the sea, where the flock can be heard burring or yapping. Their numbers are declining due to pollution from the North Sea, which has destroyed or poisoned the eel-grass that is almost their sole winter foodplant.

Across the mud in winter the waders pick their way on long thin legs, probing for small crabs, worms, shrimps, snails or shellfish. Curlews come down from the moors to join the redshank with their long red legs and beaks which can be seen in the marshes and estuaries at any time of the year.

Other winter waders that are likely to be spotted are the tiny brown and grey streaked dunlin, in dense crowds dotted on the shore or swirling like a cloud of midges over the marshes.

The little squat grey knot is also seen in huge crowds, passing through Britain in late summer on a stupendous migration journey from well inside the arctic circle to Africa, Asia and even Australia. Some knot stay on over the winter, to be rejoined by the returning travellers later in the following spring. They are usually seen either in enormous aerial crowds like dunlin, a thousand moving and changing direction as one, or all standing solemnly together at the water's edge, facing the same way into the wind.

The splendidly named bar-tailed godwit (pale grey-brown in winter, rich chestnut in summer, with dark bars on the tail) is another wanderer that passes through Britain in late summer and early spring migration flights; they can be seen on the enormous sand and mud saucer of Morecambe Bay, around the Wash, and on Romney Marsh – in fact, anywhere that muds and sands provide extensive feeding banks where they can dig up lugworms, shellfish, shrimps and sandhoppers.

The lovely and rare avocet, with its ice-blue legs, black and white plumage and a delicately upturned long bill for sweeping shrimps and water insects from the sea, can be seen in summer in its Suffolk nesting sites on Havergate Island and at Minsmere, both RSPB reserves, and on the broad estuary of the River Tamar on the Devon/Cornwall border in winter. Avocets were exterminated in

Bar Mouth, east of Castlerock, Co Derry.
Estuary with big population of nesting and overwintering birds. Birdwatching hides; facilities for disabled.

Britain by the early nineteenth century and were not seen again until 1950. Now, protected and encouraged by the RSPB, the few avocets that made a tentative reinvasion as breeding birds have increased to a small but firmly established population.

CLIFF AND SEASHORE

The final area of wildlife walking to be described is where the land finally disappears – the cliffs and sand and shingle of the seashore. One only has to move a short distance from a crowded holiday beach which is apparently lifeless (apart from humans), to find flowers and birds in abundance – where sand mounds up into dunes, where shingle is heaped and everywhere along the cliffs: all the places, in fact, where beach baskers do not go.

All over the cliffs English stonecrop makes mats of fleshy red cylindrical leaves, on which sprout tiny flowers with pointed white petals, the whole plant keeping low enough to let the sea wind whip overhead. By contrast, thrift trembles to every wind on the clifftops and in rock crevices, its tiny pale pink flowers in round blobs of heads on long stalks growing anywhere that enough soil has formed to give the slightest root-hold. Rock samphire, another plant of the cliff faces and ledges, grows taller and more sturdy than thrift with milky yellow umbellifer flowerheads and thick pointed little leaves that sprout in smooth stubs from a rubbery grey stem. For centuries it was gathered from its all but inaccessible strongholds by brave climbers, who would sell it in the local market or to London dealers; it can be eaten hot or cold after boiling, be pickled, made into a sauce, eaten raw, or be used in a salad.

On the shore, but well back from the tide, sand blows into fixed dunes which keep much the same shape from season to season. Marram grass keeps them together rather as sea purslane does the salt-marsh, with long roots that intertwine and take firm hold. The sand builds up, trapped by the marram grass. Marram is often deliberately planted to create dunes in areas of bad sea erosion. Reddish purple sand sedge does the same job. Once it is fixed and stable, the dune is a huge lime-larder for flowering plants by virtue of the broken shells and bits of dead sea creatures in its sand.

Orchids grow in the slacks or damp hollow backs of the dunes: the pyramidal orchid, bee orchid and various marsh orchids. Bloody cranesbill carpets the dunes with big crimson flowers. Sea buckthorn grows into a bush that can become the size of a small tree, with long sharp prickles that can deliver a really painful jab to the unwary rambler. In late summer it bears large bright orange berries.

Nearer the sea, on dunes that change shape with the wind and tide, ragwort grows well, as does the startlingly blue viper's bugloss. These mobile dunes may be held roughly together by long-rooted sea couch grass as well as by thinly scattered marram. Prickly saltwort's sharp-tipped leaves and prickle-covered stems

Forvie Nature Reserve, Collieston, Grampian, Scotland. Visitor Centre with exhibition on history and wildlife of these 6 square miles (15km²) of sand-dunes, moorland and cliff.

Kebble National Nature Reserve, Rathlin Island, off Ballycastle, Co Antrim. Enormous guillemot colonies on rock stacks; razorbill, shag, cormorant, puffin, black guillemot, chough, many other sea bird species.

Skomer, Skokholm and Grassholm Islands, off south-west Pembrokeshire coast, Dyfed, South-West Wales. Skomer and Skokholm: enormous colonies of Manx shearwaters; also fulmar, shag, kittiwake, puffin, guillemot, razorbill and several gull species; grey seals. Grassholm: owned by RSPB. Nearly 50,000 breeding gannets – third-largest colony in the North Atlantic.

Murlough National Nature Reserve, near Dundrum, Co Down. Sand dune system, heath and woodland, estuary and sea.

(Opposite) Sea thrift nods its pink heads wherever clefts in the cliffs hold enough soil for its roots.

Oxwich Nature Reserve, Oxwich, Gower, West Glamorgan. Visitor Centre with exhibition on the reserve: sand-dunes, fresh- and salt-water marsh, woodland and shore. Daily list of wildlife to be seen on the reserve. Excellent leaflets on all aspects of its wildlife. Nature trail through the dunes.

are found here in mats, as are the small thick oval leaves of sea sandwort that form a cowl for the tiny white flowers.

Where shingle lies flat and stable, you may see herb robert's big pink flowers, or the white ones of sea campion. Shingle banks can be heaped by one storm or high tide and redistributed by the next. They are home to several kinds of plants, all of which are extremely tolerant of salt: sea kale, with crinkly leaves like cabbage (don't bother picking them to cook – they will outlast the strongest jaw and outblast the hardiest palate – but try the boiled stems with butter); sea holly, with pale blue, spiky leathery leaves and pale blue flowers with thistle heads; and yellow-horned poppy, the petals of whose enormous poppy-like yellow flowers drop off at the merest touch.

Shelduck feed on the tideline among the herring gulls, looking for molluscs and small marine creatures to scoop up with their red bills. They are big, strikingly coloured birds, with a white breast and body, chestnut shoulders, a black head and black stripe down the wing-tip. As the tide comes in and covers the muds, the shelduck fly off to the marshes or inland fields.

Oystercatchers are unmistakable with their black upper half, white lower parts, bright pink legs and large orange nut-cracker bill with which they knock and lever open shellfish – not just oysters, but cockles and mussels, winkles, shrimps and crabs. 'Pic-pic' is their normal cry and 'kleep-kleep' their alarm call.

Turnstones patter like clockwork along the tideline, turning over the stones, seaweed and shells in the hope of finding insects or small shellfish.

Among the shingle pebbles in May and July the ringed plover (short yellow bill, brown back, black collar and stripe across the eye) scrapes together bits of broken shell to make a nest for its four stone-coloured eggs, whose dark blotches camouflage them against a stony background. If you see a plover dragging itself painfully along the shingle with an apparently broken wing trailing uselessly beside it, don't waste your sympathy on it, for almost certainly it is trying to entice you away from its nest, which may well be right under your feet.

USEFUL EQUIPMENT

To enjoy the wildlife of Britain from the mountains to the tideline, there is only one indispensable piece of equipment that you need with you on your walk – a sharp pair of eyes. The more bulky and weighty things you leave at home, the happier you will be. There are three items, though, that will increase your enjoyment wherever you are. A pair of lightweight binoculars turns a speck on wings into an identifiable bird and a blob on the skyline into a sharply outlined red deer. A small camera captures the harebell and the swallowtail butterfly just as securely as picking or killing, and leaves them still alive and in situ for the delight of the next rambler who passes that way. The flower whose size, colour, number of petals and shape of leaves were so sharp and obvious when picked will have turned into a shrivelled, colourless wisp by the time you get it home. Your photographs and notes, checked against the book description, will recreate a flower far more clearly than a picked specimen. With a notebook and pencil you can jot notes as you observe and leave the pocket-filling identification books at home to be consulted later.

IDENTIFICATION BOOKS

I have found the following books very helpful in identifying wildlife:

The Wild Flowers of Britain and Northern Europe by Richard and Alastair Fitter and Marjorie Blamey (Collins, 1974)
British Butterflies – A Field Guide by Robert Gooden (David & Charles, 1978)
A Field Guide to the Insects of Britain and Northern Europe by Michael Chinery (Collins, 1973)
A Field Guide to the Birds of Britain and Europe by Roger Peterson, Guy Mountfort and P. A. D. Hollom (3rd edition – Collins, 1974)

For out-of-the-way, entertaining information on the uses of various plants:

The Englishman's Flora by Geoffrey Grigson (Paladin, 1975)
Food for Free by Richard Mabey (Fontana, 1975)

For superb colour photographs of wild flowers:

Wild Flowers of Britain by Roger Phillips (Pan, 1977)

THE COUNTRY CODE

Finally, there is a simple and effective set of guidelines known as the Country Code. Kept in mind, they are a guarantee of enjoyment for all ramblers and lovers of the countryside and are a safeguard for wildlife everywhere.

> Guard against all risk of fire.
> Fasten all gates.
> Keep dogs under proper control.
> Keep to the paths across farmland.
> Avoid damaging fences, hedges and walls.
> Leave no litter.
> Safeguard water supplies.
> Protect wildlife, wild plants and trees.
> Go carefully on country roads.
> Respect the life of the countryside.

CHAPTER 3

THE COUNTRYSIDE
AT WORK

At the school in south Somerset where I used to teach, the countryside was an ever-popular subject for drawing, painting and modelling. The children had the material for inspiration right on their doorsteps, for their small town was set among green dairy pastures and rolling hills. No matter what the artistic talents of each child, the images of the countryside they created with their pencils, paints or clay all had the same basic components – a group of black-and-white cows with their heads down and munching in a field of grass. There might be a farmer in wellington boots, a river crammed with smiling fish of unlikely shape and colour, or (the favourite optional extra) a big pillarbox-red tractor with 'DAVID BROWN' lettered unevenly along its bonnet. But cows and grass were always there. To those Somerset children a country scene without cows and pasture fields was unthinkable.

When I moved to teach in Suffolk, however, it was corn and combine harvesters that summed up the countryside for my pupils. I often wondered what totems of the countryside would have featured in the paintings and models of schoolchildren living among the fertile soils of the Vale of Evesham, the fens of Lincolnshire or the hills of Northumberland. Would such children invariably have centred their creations on apple trees, potato prairies or sheep and sheep-dogs? And would their parents, set the same task, have been any more adventurous; or would they, too, have depicted the local kind of farming landscape as the norm?

We all know exactly what we mean when we think of the countryside; but what we think of depends very much on where we live. We are not as parochial in our outlook as were our forefathers, of course; thanks to the motor-car and the motorway, a morning's drive almost anywhere across the country, from Cornwall to way beyond the Scottish border, will put you in sight of a tremendous variety of countryside – hills, valleys, marshes, plains, woods, pasture, cornfields; the countryside of cattle, pigs, poultry, sheep, grain, fruit and vegetables. From television those Somerset children I taught were as familiar with the sight of sheep-dogs in the Yorkshire dales and combine harvesters in vast East Anglian grain fields, with Scottish mountains and Kentish marshes, as they were with their own local cows and grass. Yet cows and grass it was for them, and corn and combines for the Suffolk children, ten times out of ten, when the subject was the countryside. Cows and cornfields feature largely in the countryside notions of children who are born and bred in cities, although in the artwork of a single class you are likely to see pigs and sheep as well – oxen in a Pakistani landscape, too, or melons and sugar cane against a background of Jamaican jungle. City children, although they may only rarely find themselves in the countryside, also have strong and fixed ideas of what it looks like, ideas that are almost always based on farming.

All this is by way of saying that farms and farming loom large in our personal view of what the countryside is and how it should look – unsurprisingly, since four out of five acres in Britain are farmland of one kind or another. Notwithstanding the growth of towns and cities, the building of roads, the diggings and heapings of mines and quarries, the construction of industrial complexes and the sprawl of their wasteland, farming in its various forms still has by far the greatest influence on the countryside. The appearance of the farming countryside changes with the seasons as it has always done. The bare brown of winter ploughland and the rich gold of summer barley succeed each other in a Suffolk valley in a time-honoured round which would be instantly familiar to the present-day farmer's great-grandfather. But he would stare to see the hillside above that valley bright yellow in the spring with oil-seed rape, the criss-cross of hedges that he knew all vanished, and his wooden barn now converted into an artist's studio. The Sussex shepherd of Victorian days would be flabbergasted to return to his sheepwalks on the downs and find them under a hundred acres of corn. The fashions of farming alter through the years, and the countryside alters with them, as susceptible to change as any town or city.  Just about the only landscape resistant to the effects of modern farming is that in which the crofters of the Scottish Highlands and islands operate. Because crofting is such a small-scale operation, often carried out on a dozen or so acres in the most difficult of country, its practitioners have no hope of getting rich. With the help of fishing, crafts, bed-and-breakfast for tourists, and generous grants, they get by if they are lucky. So there is no place in crofting for the chemical spray or the huge mechanical machine, and the Highland and island landscapes benefit in consequence.

To give a detailed account of the work of all categories of British farmer would take several specialised books and turn out to be academic and indigestible reading matter. It's better, therefore, to look at how some genuine farmers, living and working in the British countryside, run their farms, and to consider some of the day-to-day pleasures and problems of modern farming.

Although the 'greenhouse effect' (discussed in Chapter 4) has already begun to make changes in our climate, the course of the four seasons still dictates the yearly working timetable of the farmer. The appearance and character of any farmer's patch of countryside still depends almost entirely on the state of the seasons and the state of the weather. Nine farmers were kind enough to open the secrets of their farms to me and describe how they run their very different operations and the activities that they are engaged in throughout the year. I looked at a dairy farm in Devon and a mixed farm below the Sussex downs; a fruit farm in the fertile Vale of Evesham; two farms in East Anglia that grow cereals and

North-East of Scotland Agricultural Heritage Centre, Aden Country Park, Old Deer, near Peterhead, Grampian, Scotland. Housed in restored Aden Home Farm. Display and interpretation of twentieth-century life on an estate: audio-visual programme, horseman's house, costume guide. Also exhibition of two hundred years of farming in north-east of Scotland.

vegetables; a sheep farm on the bleak foothills of the Cheviots, near the Scottish border; a crofting family in Britain's northernmost island; an organic farm in West Wales; and a beef farm in Northern Ireland. Each farm is different from the others, each one responding in its own way to the dictates and demands of the weather, the seasons and the ever-changing market.

JOHN AND ROSEMARY BERRY, BILLINGSMOOR FARM, DEVON
Dairy and Amenity

The rich green countryside of mid-Devon undulates into lush valleys and hedged hilltops all around Billingsmoor Farm. This is the kind of farming landscape that was so familiar to those Somerset schoolchildren I used to teach – cows and grass, cows and grass as far as the eye can see. The deep lanes between their high hedgebanks are smeared red with mud. John and Rosemary Berry farm 232 acres (94ha) which is rented from the Duchy of Cornwall and another 23 acres (9ha) which was bought as an investment – the tenure of their house may end with their retirement. They moved to Billingsmoor Farm from the neighbouring Stout Farm in 1979, at a time when British dairy farmers were prospering. But dairying was also booming all across the European farming community. There was too much milk, too much butter and too much cheese, resulting in the notorious 'lakes' and 'mountains' of food produce. Within four years of the Berrys' move they found themselves victims of the quota system. This system was designed by the EC to discourage farmers from overproducing milk by fixing the amount they can produce and penalising any overstepping of that limit. Suddenly dairy farmers found that the good times had gone. Many sold up and left dairy farming.

John and Rosemary Berry, farming where they do, had no alternative but to carry on dairying, but they decided to diversify in order to safeguard their living. Tentatively they tried the then virtually untested waters of conservation, while attempting to exploit the leisure, tourist and educational market that would grow as a result. And the experiment (which was well supported with materials and encouragement by the Duchy of Cornwall) has been successful, both financially and aesthetically. Although the 150 Friesian cows still provide the backbone of the farm's income, other enterprises have been established: educational courses and visits (which pay their way) in converted farm buildings; trout and coarse fishing in the ponds that the Berrys have dug; self-catering holidaymakers accommodated in their two modernised cottages; the sale of Christmas trees that have been grown in odd corners unsuitable for cattle grazing; the production of organic swedes, oats and wheat, and the cultivation of evening primrose for the extraction of medicinal oil. And now on Billingsmoor Farm there are more birds, animals, butterflies and wild flowers, more trees, more hedgerows and more watery areas than there were before.

John Berry drove me bumpily around the farm in his mud-encrusted Land-Rover, pointing out the carefully laid and shaped hedges, the ponds, the new plantations and the areas that have been left wild, until my sights were adjusted and I could pick out the features for myself among the fields and lanes of Billingsmoor. It was damned hard work, John told me, farming in this way, but both he and Rosemary thought that it was well worth it. One example was the control of weeds on the non-organic pastureland that makes up 80 per cent of the farm's land. Mechanical topping of the pasture destroyed the weeds, but it was not as effective as a thorough application of chemicals. If there was a very heavy infestation, they would probably resort to chemical herbicides, but they were avoiding them on a day-to-day basis. Hedges were another point: it took time, trouble and labour to lay them properly and to plant out new ones, but the return on that investment was the knowledge that the cows would stay in the right place and not be trampling crops in the next field. Those awkward little corners of fields and small areas of streamside ground in useful production, growing trees, were a satisfying sight, and it was good to see the visiting children reading, drawing and asking questions along the nature trails and education room that the Berrys have set up in the old cattle shippen.

The dairy operation has been an up-and-down affair. The Milk Marketing Board buys all the milk, paying according to its quality, standards of hygiene, butter fat and bacterial content. Too much butter fat can incur a penalty. The farmer cannot be certain if, when or how much he may be penalised in any particular year, because there are too many variables. Dry summers with poor grass mean that expensive silage, which has been made and hoarded for the hungry winter months, has to be fed to the cattle all year round.

Just before my visit there had been the BSE, or bovine spongiform encephalopathy, scare – 'Mad Cow Disease', as the newspapers rejoiced in labelling it – which had seen this appalling, brain-destroying disease cross over species from sheep to cows. Would it cross over further to human eaters of beef? No one could be sure. The prospect that humans might be susceptible to BSE, however remote, had been enough to cause beef prices to plummet. Elderly cows whose milk supply had dried up were almost valueless. The situation would probably stabilise once the media had another story to dramatise, John Berry reckoned, but it was one more area of uncertainty.

The impossibility of predicting how dairy farming will go in the future has been the biggest single influence in pushing John and Rosemary towards diversifying their farming. The position of the farm, which is isolated in a tangle of steep muddy lanes, means that there are problems in marketing their produce, but the Berrys are determined to make it work. Many farmers select conservation efforts – demanding as they are of time, labour and imaginative planning – as the first item to abandon when rising costs, falling profits and a swelling overdraft force them to economise. But John

John Berry of Billingsmoor Farm.

and Rosemary believe that the projects they have instigated, with their potential for attracting visitors and opening up new markets, offer the best future for small family farms.

Successive British governments may be set on withdrawing the grant support on which farmers have so greatly relied in the past, but there is a likelihood of assistance via the EC as a reward for cutting back on overproduction and for 'going green'. Billingsmoor Farm is an excellent advertisement for this way of looking at modern farming. John and Rosemary Berry recently won first prize in the Royal Association of British Dairy Farmers' national landscape conservation competition.

BOB PETERS, PLASHETT PARK FARM, EAST SUSSEX
Mixed Farming

You have to drive a long and bumpy way down a rutted track to reach Bob Peters' farmhouse, a solid old red-brick building that is half smothered with ivy and stands to one side of a jumble of old and new sheds and barns. A green-painted Field Marshall diesel tractor, acquired by Bob's father just after World War II, stands beside an outmoded combine harvester whose once-crimson paintwork has faded in the suns of thirty summers. In the Dutch barn lies

Friesian cows, the backbone of British dairying.

another museum-piece, a splendid wooden-sided thrashing machine that still sees action from time to time. These relics of farming times past, kept by Bob Peters because he likes them, bear witness to his approach to farming, which is careful, reliable and with a regard for tradition.

However, Bob's farming methods are not old-fashioned in a negative sense. He has been farming at Plashett Park Farm close to the downs, a couple of miles from Lewes in East Sussex, since 1952, running a farm which has changed – as all farms have done over the past forty years – in accordance with the changing demands and techniques of modern agriculture. The farm is part of a large estate and Bob rents it as a tenant. When his father was in charge there were fewer than 250 acres (100ha) to work, but as other small farmers on the estate have gone out of business, more land has been added to Bob's account. Now he works 525 acres (212ha) of heavy clay and light greensand around his farmhouse, the result of the amalgamation of four small farms, and another 132 acres (53ha) of greensand and gravel nearby.

Bob Peters manages a mixed farm consisting of a steady balance of 140 Friesian dairy cows, some beef calves that are reared for sale at 15 to 18 months as store cattle (to be fattened elsewhere for slaughter), 40 Suffolk-cross sheep that graze on pasture, 9 Gloucestershire Old Spot and Large Black sows and their piglets, a few hens to provide breakfast eggs for Bob's family, and 150 acres (60ha) of wheat, oats and barley for cattle-feed.

In Bob's father's day eight full-time farm workers were employed on a much smaller farm; when they took on contracting work on other farms, the number of workers rose to sixteen. But the rise in wages and the increased mechanisation of farm work have seen the workforce decrease to its present number of two cowmen and two tractor drivers. Between them they get all the work done, more easily but with less pleasure in the job than in the old days. 'The fun's gone out of farming,' Bob says. 'We used to get sore backs carrying two-hundredweight sacks, but there was always banter and laughing at work. Now it's just a job.'

Bob Peters has been a 'green' farmer all his life. He would not rip out a hedge, fill in a pond, burn his straw or obstruct a footpath if you paid him to do it. He likes the birds, the wild flowers and insects, and is willing to take advice from conservation bodies on how to restore nature to what has become on many neighbouring farms a very unnatural countryside. The Sussex Farming and Wildlife Advisory Group has put together a thick document advising Bob on all kinds of conservation matters – woodlands, ponds, ditches, grasslands, hedges; on establishing new habitats and creating a farm trail. He is in agreement with all their ideas; but without the nitrogen and compound fertilisers drilled into the soil with the corn and the weedkillers sprayed on the crops, he could see himself going out of business in a short time.

However, Bob uses as few artificial chemicals as possible and is content to reap 2 tons of corn per acre instead of the 3 or 4 he might have if he drenched his land with chemicals. Bob understands, even if he does not condone, the chemical farming of some farmers. 'It's a question of priorities and economics. When something has to be cut back, the green outlook, the conservation, is always the first thing to go. The price has to be right before farmers will be conservationists, and prices have been dropping all the way round.'

The scare over BSE has hit all cattle farmers hard. So have the restrictions and penalties of the milk quota. Times are tough – harder even than in the agricultural depression of the 1930s which caused Bob's father so much suffering. 'After that recession,' Bob told me, 'the farms were still there, a bit neglected, but still capable of being put back in order. But now they are converting the farm-houses into nice residences for commuters and building on the farmland. Development – always development. The farms them-selves just won't be there when this recession comes to an end.'

PAUL DUNSBY, VALE OF EVESHAM
Fruit

Paul Dunsby's orchards cover 100 acres (40ha) in the Vale of Evesham, one of the best fruit-growing areas in Britain with its sheltered central position and heavy clay soil. These hundred acres lie mostly on gentle hill slopes above the vale's green pastures. The orchards have expanded greatly since Paul Dunsby's father started the business after World War II with just 2 acres (0.8ha) of apple trees and a self-built bungalow. Paul himself has been in charge of the operation for the best part of forty years, gradually buying up land in small parcels whenever it becomes available. Such a business swallows a large amount of capital: to buy 15 acres (6ha) of land, plant it with trees and bring them into production might tie up £50,000–70,000 over four years. And the trees have to be replaced every twenty years or so.

The orchards grow mostly Cox apples, a positive winner with the supermarkets who take almost all of Paul's crop. Supermarkets, unlike market-stall traders, want only the best – class 1 fruit, unblemished, as perfect as it can be – and pay top price for it. Cox's are sweet, crisp and good-looking – 'the Rolls-Royce of apples', as Paul says. Of the 100 acres (40ha), 80 (32ha) are planted with Cox's; another 5 acres (2ha) are planted with rougher, tougher varieties, chiefly Malus or wild crab-apples. The crab-apple trees are scattered throughout the Cox's like gypsies at Ascot, their pollen cross-fertilising the Cox's and bringing a hardy strain to that over-bred aristocrat among apples.

The remainder of the trees in Paul Dunsby's orchard, apart from a few Bramley cooking apples, are Victoria plums, which are heavy and sweet. In the 1970s the Dunsbys grew a lot of small tasteless plums for canning, but tinned fruit has fallen out of fashion and people now want natural produce on their tables.

Apples and plums are the heart of Paul's business. He provides

Bob Peters of Plashett Park Farm.

steady work to a small number of men and a few local women in his cold-store and packing shed. But most of the work, especially the picking, is done by casual labour, students on their holidays or vale women wanting a few weeks' extra money. They come to the orchards in August and are finished by the end of September. The best of the fruit they pick goes to the supermarkets. The remaining fruit, if it can be graded as class 2 – the same eating value as the supermarket variety but perhaps slightly bruised or blemished – is sold to the wholesale market, and sold on across market stalls or greengrocers' counters.

Like all fruit growers, Paul Dunsby is engaged in a constant battle with a host of enemies – diseases, insects, fungi, frosts. Cox's apples are highly susceptible to all of these problems. Scab blotches them; codling moth eggs hatch maggots that bore into them; fungus blights them; frost nips their buds. To combat the insects, diseases and fungi there are chemical sprays and Paul uses them with no particular qualms. He remembers the days when, without wearing protective clothing, he would happily spray such concoctions as nicotine, DDT and lead arsenic. He reckons that modern chemicals are safe in comparison. 'Which would you rather have?' he asks rhetorically. 'A dirty great maggot in your plum, or a minute amount

(Opposite) Picking apples – the supermarkets want the best.

of chemical?' Most of the chemicals he uses are sprayed on the tree before the fruit develops, and the dilution – one wine-glass of chemical to 250gal (1,140 litres) of water – means that only the tiniest trace actually reaches the fruit: a trace that is undetectable by scientists, says Paul.

Paul Dunsby has little time for green watchdogs who talk about chemicals in fruit; he believes that their advice is mainly a fuss about nothing. He does not lay the blame for the disappearance of birds and butterflies – which he acknowledges has happened – on sprayed chemicals, but on hedge-ripping and Dutch elm disease, which have removed natural cover and increased wind-blow. He has an ongoing programme of reinstating hedges and planting poplars and elders on his own land to help local wildlife to re-establish itself, which he is confident will happen sooner or later.

JAMES STAMPER, WEST FARM, SUFFOLK/NORFOLK BORDER
Mixed Arable

When James Stamper's grandfather moved in 1930 from the Cumbrian hills to the flat country of the Breckland, he had to break his way into virgin heath. Breckland straddles the border of Norfolk and Suffolk, a difficult land of deep, coarse sand with underlying chalk. The whole area had been a barren waste of rabbit warrens and scrub for centuries, until the Forestry Commission began to plant it with conifers shortly after World War I. These days the Breckland forests cover nearly 100 square miles (260km²), among which the arable farms have carved wide swaths in the dry old heath. Drought is the biggest problem here, although you would not suspect it as you look over the bursting acres of corn and sugar beet. What nature could not achieve, modern agricultural chemicals and methods, together with clever irrigation, have managed.

James Stamper has managed West Farm since 1961 as a tenant of two neighbouring estates, farming about 1,500 acres (600ha) these days. He is a modern farmer in every sense, a confident champion of up-to-date techniques who sees his job as a business. He is happy to use whatever tools technology and science can put in his hand to help the farm achieve greater productivity. In combating the East Anglian farmer's problem of windblow (the drying up and blowing away of topsoil) James has tried one method after another – wet furrow pressing, which corrugates the soil into hard, windproof peaks; spraying an artificial plastic-oil coat of Vynamol to bind the soil together; planting a cover crop of barley which has been burned off with another chemical a few inches above the ground to provide shelter for the young plants. He will give any new method of which he approves a trial on the farm. His combine harvester contains £30,000 worth of electronic gadgetry which monitors the yield of every 33ft (10m) stretch of ground and programmes a microchip with the information. The chip, which is inserted in his electronically equipped sprayer, ensures that the poorer ground receives less fertiliser, thus cutting down waste. Monitoring every aspect of the farm's work, planning ahead, predicting budgets, keeping production costs low, ordering expensive machinery well ahead of delivery date to obtain a good discount – these are more the stuff of farming to James than any yeoman thumb dug in the ground or weather-eye cocked on the clouds.

The productivity of West Farm bears witness to the success of this business-like outlook. On James Stamper's 1,500 acres (600ha) grow winter and spring wheat for animal feed, milling and distilling; barley for malting and seed; oil-seed rape for domestic oil; sugar beet to be converted into high-grade sugar in the factory at Bury St Edmunds; potatoes and parsnips; lettuces for supermarkets and carrots for canning. Only the dryness of the soil limits the farm's output. A specialist grower-seller pays James a fee and provides the machinery to produce the potatoes and other vegetables, but the cereal crops and sugar beet are the Stampers' own concern. The beet harvester is also electronically controlled and can lift 700 tons of beet off 30 acres (12ha) in a single day. All this is achieved with the help of just two workers and James's son, Angus. After an hour or two on the Stampers' farm, one is ready to believe that the whole of British agriculture would collapse if they ever went out of business.

Successful as the farm is, its crops are as susceptible to devastation by insects, disease, fungus and weeds as anywhere else. James Stamper wields his sprayers against all these enemies, using sufficient spray to produce his crops economically. Typically, he has the statistics in his head: 98 per cent of the spray hits the target, making it as ecologically viable as he thinks realistically it can be. Pesticides deal with the aphids that suck the goodness from the grain seeds and transmit the exotic-sounding 'barley yellow dwarf' virus. Fungicides wipe out mildew and the brown and yellow rust that can reduce a cereal crop by 75 per cent. Herbicides extirpate the thistles, docks, mayweed, bindweed and rogue grasses that EC rules stipulate shall not form more than 2 per cent of any crop delivered to port.

James says that he has not noticed any significant reduction in the wildlife on West Farm during his tenure, although the proximity of so many tens of thousands of woodland acres must help to maintain it. Breckland has been designated an ESA (Environmentally Sensitive Area) and the farm keeps 13 acres (5ha) of wet grassland untouched as natural habitat. On one section, by agreement with the landlord, a 20ft (6m) headland is left around the edge of each field as a wildlife refuge.

James has made other efforts towards conservation: only 600ft (180m) of hedgerow have been removed in his time, while shelter belts of mixed soft- and hardwoods have been planted against the windblow that the continuous felling of the surrounding forests will bring. He cuts all his hedges personally, leaving them 6ft (1.8m) high and 2ft (0.6m) wide to provide animal passageways at their roots, and does the trimming in late winter before the birds have begun to nest and while berries and seeds are still unsprouted.

This forethought and careful planning are second nature to a man who is deeply immersed in farming politics through the National Farmers' Union and the Tenants' Committee, of which he is vice-chairman. James is well aware of the poor image that the general public has of farmers and of the difficulty that many farmers are experiencing in remaining in business. He believes that they have brought most of these difficulties on themselves, through over-borrowing at the bank, purchase of land at unrealistic prices, persistence with rule-of-thumb farming techniques, and, most of all, through a failure to monitor their own operations, collect the statistics, draw conclusions and apply them.

James's son, Angus, has as good a business head as his father and provides him with a flow of information. The fax machine in the farm office plays as important a part in the success of the farm as the tractor and seed drill. 'Here in the office is where the profits are made,' says James Stamper. 'Angus and I are both more use in here than out there on a tractor. The computer in the combine will use a

James Stamper of West Farm.

satellite link as soon as they can get the blessed thing up there. Information from all over the country will be beamed into a central computer in Warwickshire and sent on here by fax. We'll have the results in half an hour. That's the way farming is today, like it or not.'

JULIAN PROCTOR, ONSLOW FARM, LINCOLNSHIRE
Mixed Arable

Julian Proctor's 635 acre (257ha) farm is a modern one and as diverse as that of James Stamper. Potatoes, wheat, sugar beet, peas, oil-seed rape, onions and green vegetables all grow on Onslow Farm. They thrive in such profusion because on the edge of the Wash the totally flat land is about the best in the British Isles. At one time in history all this fenland area of East Anglia lay either under the sea itself or – as in the case of Onslow Farm – under a boggy morass of marsh, reeds and water. Partly reclaimed by the Romans and partly by medieval monks, drained by the seventeenth-century Dutch water engineers and assiduously cultivated by the fen farmers, these flat miles of Grade 1 silt produce the corn and vegetables that end up on supermarket shelves all across the country.

When Julian's great-great-uncle began farming in Lincolnshire in 1860 there were probably forty or fifty men, women and children working these 600-odd acres. Every task, from sowing the seed to harvesting the crop, from laying drainage pipes to humping sacks into place in the barn, had to be done by hand with basic manual farming tools. Nowadays things are very different. It takes only six employees to do the work of fifty, thanks to the technology that has revolutionised twentieth-century farming. Even since 1964, when Julian Proctor began farming, there have been enormous changes. Horses still shared haulage duties with tractors when he started, but they have all gone now. The number of man-hours absorbed by the land has fallen by three-quarters. Drills and planters, ploughs and enormous harvesters, sprayers and loaders, hedge and grass mowers, cultivators and a clutch of tractors sweep through the work that once bent many Lincolnshire backs. The great fields of rich black soil – the biggest are 40 acres (16ha) – produce far more food than Julian's great-great-uncle could ever have dreamed of, yet they absorb incalculably less labour. What they do absorb, however, is a mixture of more than sixty judiciously applied agricultural chemicals. It takes nineteen kinds of herbicide to enable those acres to produce the volume of crop that is demanded by the ever-hungrier market.

Onslow Farm may be more productive today than it was a hundred years ago, but it is a rather less interesting place to work. The fruit harvest that once formed a part of its economy has been abandoned and cows are no longer seen on the farm. However, there has been a big increase in the quality of all the produce. The public expects high-quality produce these days – no blemishes, no under-sized ones and no sign of rot – and the supermarket buyers demand it. Although they have brought about the quality boom, the super-markets and their critical buyers are Julian's biggest headache. All farmers of any size in the area who want to stay in business have to deal with the supermarkets; and, as with Paul Dunsby's apples grown in the Vale of Evesham, the buyers only want the best. It is impossible to haggle with the supermarkets' buyers and unviable to look elsewhere for an outlet for the farm's produce. Backed up by their enormous wealth, the supermarkets set the agenda on prices, on crop types, on quality and quantity. It is their requirements that dictate the shape, appearance and character of the fenland farming countryside today. Julian Proctor, for example, grows 80 acres (32ha) of potatoes, 70 acres (28ha) of peas, 30 acres (12ha) of onions and 15 acres (6ha) of greenstuff – amounts that are carefully tailored to what the supermarkets will buy.

Within these constraints, however, Julian is carrying out what conservation measures he can. Hedge-ripping is the most notorious sin of the fenland farmers in their drive to increase field size in response to the increasing size of farm machinery. Since World War II 800yd (730m) of hedgerow have been removed from Onslow Farm, but another 5,000yd (4,600m) have been planted. Julian does not want to see his topsoil drying up and blowing away and he likes to see the birds and animals that have fled so much of the East Anglian prairieland. Therefore the hedges are allowed to grow much as nature dictates and are trimmed as lightly as possible. The drainage dykes that form the margins of the fields are left unmown until August so that the reeds and grasses can give shelter to nesting birds and their young, to butterflies and small mammals. And in 1988 Julian planted 13 acres (5ha) of mixed woodland – oak, ash and Corsican pine. The supermarkets have to be satisfied and technology has to be applied to keep them supplied, but that does not have to result in a landscape that is devoid of all its natural inhabitants.

JERRY HARDING, PENTOOD UCHAF, WEST WALES
Organic Farming

Jerry Harding farms a long way out in the west of Wales, in the undulating landscape of woodland and river valleys near Cardigan in Dyfed. From the loamy soil Jerry produces potatoes and brassicas (cabbage and related vegetables) as well as beef, turkeys and eggs. Farming at Pentood Uchaf is hard work – harder, perhaps, than for many of Jerry's neighbours, for he is an organic farmer. There are no chemicals in use on his 88½ acres, no battery sheds nor animal forcing houses. Fertilising is done by means of an occasional application of ground limestone and rock phosphate, together with liberal doses of farmyard manure and a spray of liquid seaweed. Disease, weeds and the depredations of insects are dealt with by rigorous cultivation of the land, and by rotating the crops to allow variations in demands on the soil.

Jerry sells his produce through a number of organic farmers' organisations, trying to compete in the marketplace with farmers so heavily subsidised and so productive through use of agrichemicals that they often sell their meat and vegetables at prices below what it costs to produce them.

Pentood Uchaf has been farmed in this way by Jerry for seven years. Before he took it over the farm was in full-scale production of barley, with its grassland let to neighbouring farmers. Now it looks very different – many of the hedges and banks allowed to run wild, others carefully managed to provide maximum cover and feeding for wildlife, areas of scrub, scrape and rough grazing. There is no chemically-produced, artificially shiny greenness about the crops.

If Jerry Harding could have his way, this is the shape that all British farms would be in, producing delicious, chemical-free food at realistic prices rather higher than today's subsidised ones. Jerry is a passionate supporter of the Soil Association, a body that tries to fight an increasingly difficult battle against the more pernicious of modern farming methods. The Soil Association sets standards for produce which its members are obliged to meet, but these standards are not dictated by the demands of the supermarkets, nor by the makers of agrichemicals. The Association's aim is to educate the public about exactly what goes into the soil, the animals, the vegetables, the fruit, the water and the feed on the farm, and about the effects of chemicals on health.

Jerry is entirely in agreement with these ideals. 'There's a need to investigate in detail the link between pesticides and chemicals and the way that man's immune system seems to have broken down in recent years,' he says, 'but I doubt if it will ever be done in this country.'

Jerry's is one of the voices crying in the wilderness of modern British agriculture, sounding a warning note to the next generation. 'I do think,' he told me, 'that we are on the verge of destroying most of our rural social structure, especially in the less populated areas, in the interest of "efficiency" – in other words, producing food we don't need with no clear guidelines from the Government. Agribusiness uses all these drugs, chemicals, pesticides and so on to create huge volumes of produce. It's only marginally profitable, and it can't be sustained in the long run. But I'm afraid that modern agriculture is hooked on the use of chemicals and on over-production. Somehow we have to change, and develop a better understanding of the relationship between soil, health and man.'

BILL RICHARDSON, HIGH SHAW FARM, NORTHUMBERLAND
Sheep

In the Cheviot foothills near the Scottish Border, on the long saddle of ground between Redesdale and Coquetdale, Bill Richardson and his son Max run nearly 2,000 sheep on their 4,000 acres (1,600ha) of Northumbrian moor and hill. All the land lies between 700 and 1,000ft (215–300m) – high and hard country of heathery hillsides and mossy stream bottoms. The Army has several firing ranges in

the area, but men work and sheep feed without even turning their heads as the distant bangs and crumps go off. Bill himself should be used to loud noises, as he was a policeman in wartime London and Bradford.

The Richardsons are descended from a long line of Cumbrians. The family moved to Northumberland in 1950, since when they have established a highly successful sheep farm. Bill worked with sheep all through his boyhood in the South Tyne Valley, earning his pocket money skinning carcasses, driving lambs to market and netting grouse which were sent north by train to stock Scottish grouse moors. It was a tough life, but one that stood him in good stead, both as a policeman in rough city areas and as a farmer in some of the most difficult country in England.

Winter bites hard in Northumberland, with snow lying for weeks in drifts that can bury sheep. High Shaw farmhouse is at least 2 miles (3km) from anything the map would deign to call a road, and when the winding track is blocked with snow or glazed with ice it

(Opposite) Potato harvesting – methods have changed since this photograph was taken in Jersey in 1973.

Sheep are the staple of farming on the high ground of northern Britain.

can be a terrible struggle to get sheep out to market and supplies in to the farm. All the Richardsons' operations cost more and demand more planning and forethought than those of more favoured farmers 'in-bye' (down in the lowlands). There is the social isolation, too, which is exacerbated these days by the gradual victory of television over the old sociable Northumberland customs: visits, chats, get-togethers and impromptu musical sessions in the back kitchen.

The land itself is not easy. At least half the farm is made up of peat bogs and soft ground, while most of the rest rolls upward in exposed shoulders and saddles of heather and rough grass. The natural asset of these hills which makes them viable as sheep runs is the prevalence of the downy-topped cotton grass, which the Cheviot sheep farmers call 'draw moss'. The sheep draw it out of the ground and eat the white protein-rich root. Draw moss has kept the sheep on these Cheviot slopes for many centuries. The first properly organised farms were laid out in 1,000-acre (400-ha) units by the Percy and Umfraville families who dominated the area and each farm was sited to provide it with three essential commodities – water, shelter and draw moss.

Nowadays an even more vital commodity is grant money. There are subsidies for farming sheep in the hills and for farming in a 'less favoured area'. There is a 'premium' from the EC for being involved with sheep in the first place. There is also a subsidy for farming on land at over 1,000ft (305m), although the Richardsons do not benefit particularly from it.

Blackface sheep are most common in the area, but Bill Richardson prefers the Swaledales that he was brought up with. He likes their long legs, their hardiness and their short coats which ball up less readily in snow conditions than the Blackfaces'. Swaledale wool has more 'kemp', or fibrous matter. It dries out more quickly after rain, helping the sheep to retain body heat. In short, Swaledales are a better quality sheep with better wool. Bill has bred them through many generations into a race of tough beasts that lamb easily, are inherent milkers and natural foragers and stand up stoutly to the rigours of life on the hill. 'Look for open feet, good teeth and a bright eye, my father always said,' Bill remembers, 'and that's not bad advice at all.' By day the sheep graze the valley bottoms and are driven to the hilltops in order to stay cool and to avoid over-grazing of the richer grass and draw moss lower down. The Richardsons can handle all the day-to-day work themselves, aided by their five home-bred Border collie dogs, but they hire contractors for shearing and dipping, and for fencing work.

Remoteness is one of the problems of this kind of farming, as already noted; harsh winter weather is another. An unruly dog among the sheep at lambing time can cause havoc, too. But the main enemies are the sheep diseases and pests in their various forms: keds (spider-like creatures that feed on the sheep's skin, causing maddening irritation); lice; blowfly maggots that can eat a sheep alive; bloodsucking ticks; worms; sheep scab. Bill prefers to treat these pests at source and by natural methods. He burns the heather and limes the hillside (there is a subsidy available for this) to kill off ticks before they ever invade their hostesses, and keeps ewes free from worms by rotational grazing which breaks the parasite's life cycle. He is pleased to see the emergence of a new form of environmentally friendly sheep-dip against scab, which can put an end to the use of the organophosphorous sheep scab dips prescribed by the Ministry of Agriculture that leached into the waterways and killed everything they touched.

Like most of his neighbours, Bill enjoys attending the local sheep shows, partly to compare progress and pick up new ideas, partly to socialise and swap news and views. But he has little time for the frivolity that transforms sensible beasts into the unnatural objects displayed at some of these shows – plucking hairs from faces to make appealing colour patterns, altering the shape of horns to achieve perfect symmetry, painting out unsightly blotches on legs, putting chemically induced purl in the fleeces and clipping them into a square box of wool. If sheep are bred carefully enough, Bill thinks, and if the farmer knows his business, the animals should be left to get on with their lives and to fend for themselves.

Border Collie and Shepherd Centre, Tweedhopefoot, Tweedsmuir, Borders, Scotland. Photographic exhibition of shepherds, sheep and dogs, housed in building of smallest school in Scotland (closed 1937). Craft shop in shepherd's bothy. Demonstrations of sheepdog handling.

KEVIN McAULEY, McAULEY'S FARM, CO ANTRIM, NORTHERN IRELAND
Beef

Kevin McAuley's farm in County Antrim has been in his family's ownership since 1835, so many years that it doesn't have a name of its own. 'McAuley's' is how everyone in the neighbourhood knows it. It's a well-to-do farm, at 550 acres rather a giant among the nearby small farms of between twenty and sixty acres. Kevin runs about 400 cattle on his farm – 160 suckler cows with their offspring, and up to 100 store cattle which he buys in the autumn sales and fattens in his sheds through the winter to sell at a profit in the spring. The local abattoirs and meat plants take most of the animals off his hands, though not always at a price he likes: with over-production of beef so prevalent these days, a lot of cattle are bought at a fixed and non-negotiable 'intervention' price.

A great deal of expertise, care and thought goes into the breeding of cattle on McAuley's Farm. Up till very recently Kevin's cows were a cross between Friesian and Aberdeen Angus, mated with a Charolais or Simmental bull. Now research has suggested that stronger, faster-growing and better-tasting calves may be forthcoming from a union between the same types of bull and a cow that is a cross between Friesian and either Simmental or Limousin. So Kevin is trying out the new combination. Improvements are always being sought by beef farmers from these different concoctions of blood and genes, subtly stirred and blended by the genetic engineering cooks.

Kevin feeds his cattle no artificial foods – they eat only grass, barley and maize glutin, along with the winter silage. He is doing his bit for a greener environment, too, leaving wooded areas of the farm untouched as wildlife refuges. But the recent pressures of rising costs and ever-diminishing returns, the fixed 'intervention' prices as a penalty for over-production, the drying up of grants and the tighter controls on pollution and environmental damage have made beef farming a more worrying and potentially unprofitable business than ever it used to be. Kevin can well see the need for the environmental safeguards and the deterrents to over-production, but even he, in many ways the model modern farmer, is feeling the squeeze of tighter money and heavier external controls.

'I think the outlook for beef farming is very poor,' is the gloomy assessment of Kevin, normally a warm and cheerful man, 'because of the new EC regulations for controlling our output, in particular, and the prospect of having to compete against cheap imports of beef from Eastern Europe now that the Iron Curtain's down. Fewer people are eating beef, anyway, because of the BSE scare. The whole operation's becoming much more expensive, with these very high interest rates, while the returns are getting steadily less. I couldn't say what the future of beef farming is, but it does look very uncertain.'

TONY AND IRENE MOUAT, CLINGERA, ISLAND OF UNST, SHETLAND
Crofting

The 250 acres (107ha) that make up Tony and Irene Mouat's croft are quite unlike the land of any of the other farmers we have looked at. Clingera lies along the narrow inlet of Baltasound, only a few miles from the northernmost point of Britain. This is wild, harsh country of peat moors and heathery slopes, where gales come whistling across most days of the year. Almost all of the croft is rough grazing for the Mouats' sheep and their small herd of Shetland ponies, with just a patch or two cultivated for potatoes and other vegetables, and some land under hay to supply the sheep with winter feed. There are hens on the croft to provide eggs for Tony, Irene and their two small sons, and for the bed-and-breakfast guests who stay under Clingera's hospitable roof.

Crofters have to diversify in order to make a living. No one can exist entirely on the produce of the croft these days, if indeed they ever did. 'Crofters don't get rich,' they say in Shetland, 'they get by, if they're lucky.' The Mouats are typical of modern crofters in the number of activities they turn their hands to. Tony Mouat works as a seaman on the tugs that guide giant tankers in and out of the North Sea oil terminal at nearby Sullom Voe. He also helps neighbours with their sheep and does a bit of fishing and practical building. Tony planned and built Clingera by himself. Irene runs the bed-and-breakfast business as well as taking on her full share of work around the croft and acting as unpaid taxi service to the boys. Meals at Clingera are superbly tasty, with fresh vegetables from the croft complementing the home-reared lamb.

Croft on North Uist, Outer Hebrides. With fishing, knitting, crafts and other sidelines, today's crofter can just about make a living, supported by grants.

The croft's agriculture, small-scale though it may be, is no longer managed entirely by hand, as it was when Irene Mouat was a girl. Hay is baled and silage made by tractor-driven machinery these days. On the crofts of Unst there are fewer of the house cows that used to supply creamy milk for the crofter's table. But there has been a big increase in the number of sheep: they are more profitable. For crofters in the remote northern islands of Shetland, however, high freight costs absorb a good proportion of the proceeds of their lamb sales at Aberdeen market 200 miles to the south.

Crofting is heavily subsidised by the Department of Agriculture with grants for fencing, drainage and other improvements, as well as by EC money and by preferential rates on loans, mortgages and so on. Without this extra financial underpinning it is extremely doubtful if any crofters could afford to carry on in the remoter areas of the Scottish Highlands and islands.

Yet the Mouats would not want to change their way of life. At Clingera they are free of most outside pressures, of interference by 'powers-that-be'. This precious independence is probably the chief benefit the crofters reap from their wind-scoured, lonely acres.

THE FARMING YEAR

	John and Rosemary Berry, Billingsmoor Farm, Devon – Dairy and Amenity	Bob Peters, Plashett Park Farm, Sussex – Mixed Farming	Paul Dunsby, Vale of Evesham – Fruit	James Stamper, West Farm, Suffolk/ Norfolk border – Mixed Arable
January	Cows are indoors or in yard and need milking and cleaning out. Some cows are calving. Some ewes are lambing and need feeding. Service farm equipment and order seed for spring sowing.	Clean cattle yards. Feed silage, hay, straw to cattle in yard. Some early lambing. Field work: hedging and ditching.	Hope for a good frost to slow trees into dormancy and give them a proper rest. Wash trees with tar oil to kill insect eggs. Start pruning and planting. Wash, dry, sort and pack stored apples for supermarket.	Staff holidays. Machinery maintenance.
February	Milk, calve, feed and muck out cows. Lamb some ewes. Order and take delivery of fertiliser. Repairs around farm.	Cleaning and feeding cows. Continue field work; roll new grass.	Plant more new trees. Continue washing old trees. Sort and pack more cold-store apples.	Ploughing for spring crops. Cut hedges now, before nesting begins.
March	Continue with milking, calving and muck-spreading. Feed frost-bitten swedes to cows. Lamb ewes and sell some at Exeter market. Calves to market. Harrow, roll and fertilise grass ground.	Lambing. Drill spring barley on lighter land.	Last wash for trees. Continue with apple packing and sending to supermarket.	Plant sugar beet, parsnips and spring barley. First applications of herbicide.
April	Milking, calving, cleaning cubicles. Cows now out on grass at night. Ewes and lambs to market. Roll grass. Spread fertiliser for silage and grazing.	Mid-month: cows out on grass. Spread fertiliser on grass. Drill spring barley on heavier land.	Mid-month: plum blossom shows. Spray insecticides against caterpillar and aphids; fungicide against scab and mildew; foliofeed (seaweed extract) and calcium against bitterpit disease.	Plant beet, carrots, lettuces. Continue with herbicide and apply first fungicide.
May	Milking, calving. Cows out on grass all the time. Shear sheep. Reseed land (under organic oats) to grass. Plough, muck and sow field for kale.	Clean out yards. Make silage. Sow maize for cattle feed. Spray corn with herbicide.	Finish winter pruning. Tie down branches to shape trees. Mow orchards to make grass mulch for trees.	Sugar beet and vegetable shoots are up. Continue with herbicide on these, insecticide on cereals, fungicide on potatoes.
June	Milking; end of calving. Fertilise cattle grazing ground. Cut grass for silage. Clean out old buildings and cattle sheds. Clean slurry pit and spread slurry. Farm Open Days and school visits – take children on farm tours.	Finish silage making by middle of the month. Haymaking.	Summer pruning: remove unwanted growth and let light in to centre of tree to give good colour to fruit.	Buildings maintenance. Repair machinery, prepare vehicles, clean and fumigate grain store in readiness for harvest.

Julian Proctor, Onslow Farm, Lincolnshire – Mixed Arable	Jerry Harding, Pentood Uchaf, West Wales – Organic Farming	Bill Richardson, High Shaw Farm, Northumberland – Sheep	Kevin McAuley, McAuley's Farm, County Antrim, N. Ireland – Beef	Tony and Irene Mouat, Clingera, Island of Unst, Shetland – Crofting
Maintenance work in workshop. Take stored sugar beet to factory. Staff holidays.	Feeding and strawing down housed livestock and chickens. Detailed planning for the year; outline planning for next 3½ years.	Ewes are in lamb. Feed them supplement if there is snow; otherwise they eat draw moss. Too much feeding by farmer stops sheep building up their strength by foraging. Sheep with good muscle tone can usually lamb without assistance.	Feeding cattle indoors – try to get some slurry out.	Feeding silage or hay to sheep.
Continue work in workshop. Train employees in use of farm machinery.	Ploughing. Feeding and work with livestock and chickens. Sometimes planting and other field work.	Keep careful eye on some ewes in lamb who are weak – usually 'two-shears' (3-year-olds having their second lamb). Scan sheep for those carrying twins, who need extra feed.	Cattle feeding – move slurry.	Feeding silage or hay to sheep. Dosing sheep.
Drill peas and sugar beet. Fertilise crop.	Cultivating, planting, sowing. Continue with stock work and chickens.	Feed ewes in lamb with molasses and balanced minerals.	Cattle feeding – slurry removal. Spring calving herd starts to calve.	Feeding silage or hay to sheep; also concentrates before lambing.
Plant potatoes. Spray herbicides, fungicides, insecticides.	Cultivating, planting, sowing. Fencing – stock are now out to grass. Chickens.	Lambing from mid-month. Two-shear and older ewes lamb on their own on the hill. No lambing in sheds – ewes need solitude. Castrate male lambs within first 7 days of life.	Lambing ewes, calving cows. Spread fertiliser. Roll fields; turn cattle out to grass.	Feeding and dosing sheep. Lambing starts at the end of the month.
Continue with herbicides, fungicides, insecticides.	Weeding. Silage making, planting. Preparation for harvest. Checking stock and chickens.	Lambing till end of the month.	Spraying weeds. Start silage cutting at end of the month.	Lambing.
Continue with herbicides, fungicides, insecticides. Prepare machines for harvest. Some staff holidays. Plan next year's cropping.	Cultivating through the crops, weeding, planting. Silage making. Harvest potatoes, cabbage. Check stock, chickens.	Treat all lambs in fields for internal parasites. Lambs on hill need no treatment.	Finish silage cutting. Spread fertiliser and remaining slurry.	Not much agricultural activity – hope for some tourists!

THE FARMING YEAR

	John and Rosemary Berry	Bob Peters	Paul Dunsby	James Stamper
July	Milking. Worm young cattle. Staff holiday; own holiday. Cut grass for round-bale silage. Fertilise cattle grazing ground. School visits – farm tours. Enlarge pheasant pen and take delivery of 100 six-week-old pheasants.	Heifers start calving. Haymaking. Harvest winter barley towards end of month.	Continue summer pruning. June and July are the quiet months.	From about 10th, harvest winter barley and oil-seed rape.
August	Milking. Cows finish stubble turnips, start on kale and round-bale silage. Cut grass; make hay. Make round-bale silage. Buy and worm ewes. Dip sheep. Show WI party around farm.	Continue harvest; 2 men cope where Bob's father had 8 and casual labour as well.	12th: begin picking Discovery apples (the earliest). Pick plums from mid-month.	Harvest spring barley, winter and spring wheat. Straw chopped up while combining. Post-harvest cultivation: disc the ground to help weed seeds germinate. Plough and drill oil-seed rape.
September	Milking, calving. Cows continue on round-bale silage and kale. Spread 2 loads of muck a day. Harrow and roll stubble turnip field. Spread last of fertiliser. Put ram with ewes. Show parties around farm.	Finish harvest. Clear straw, cultivate stubble. Harvest maize. Plough winter oats.	Continue picking plums till mid-month. From about 20th, pick Cox's apples – all within 2 weeks. Pick into square wooden bins and take to cold-store.	From middle of month, plough and drill winter barley and wheat. Begin to harvest sugar beet. Contract to harvest other farmers' beet.
October	Milking, calving. Cows finish kale, start on silage from pit. Cows begin to sleep indoors at night; repair cubicles. Plough kale field and sow with rye-corn for cows next spring. Maintenance: hang gates, etc. Dip sheep.	Sow winter barley and wheat. Make maize silage.	Finish picking last Cox's; all into cold-store. Controlled oxygen, CO_2, temperature and atmosphere all help to preserve fruit.	Continue harvesting own and others' sugar beet. Plough and drill winter wheat.
November	Milking, calving. Bring young cattle into sheds for winter; feed twice a day; worm. Spread 3 loads of muck a day from cubicles. Bring in lamb ewes and worm. Trim hedges. Market Christmas trees.	Finish late wheat sowing.	Begin to take fruit out of cold-store – people want fruit when winter sets in. Wash, dry, sort, grade for size and quality, pack and send to supermarket.	Continue harvesting sugar beet. Plough and drill spring wheat, which fixes nitrates in soil.
December	Milking, calving. Cows eating silage and straw. Start lambing. Worm all sheep. Market Christmas trees; local people come and choose their own. Staff holiday.	Finish all ploughing by Christmas to let frosts get at the soil – break it up and kill pests.	Continue taking fruit from cold-store, preparing and sending it to supermarket.	Finish harvesting sugar beet. From 20th onwards, farm shuts down for Christmas.

Julian Proctor	Jerry Harding	Bill Richardson	Kevin McAuley	Tony and Irene Mouat
Harvest peas and oil-seed rape.	Planting, weeding, silage making. Harvest vegetables. Checking stock, chickens. Muck spreading.	Shearing from 15th onwards.	Start calving autumn suckler herd. Put in second cut of silage; then sow fertiliser.	Clipping sheep. Dosing all sheep and lambs.
Harvest cereals.	Harvesting, sowing cash crops. Stock work; chickens, turkeys.	Haymaking. Silage making.	Reseed any fields which need it. Finish off any reclamation and drainage work. Repair or renew fences.	Hay or silage making.
Harvest potatoes and onions.	Harvesting. Winter supplies collection – straw, etc. Stock work; chickens, turkeys.	Sheep sales. Sell wether lambs (castrated males) for meat; sell draft ewes (6 years old) to in-bye (lowland) farmers for 3 more years of breeding. Sell female lambs not needed for flock maintenance.	Repair and wash cattle houses in preparation for winter. Attend cattle sales to buy store cattle for winter housing.	Gathering lambs to send to Aberdeen market. Dipping all sheep.
Harvest potatoes and sugar beet. Plough and drill winter wheat.	Harvesting. Preparing for winter. Poultry.	Buy rams from sales. Look for open feet and short black teeth set close together – these won't break on heather and coarse grasses.	Start putting cattle into sheds, and open silos.	Removing all lambs from ewes to keep over winter. Dosing sheep.
Plough and drill winter wheat. Deliver sugar beet to the factory.	Harvesting. Preparing for winter. Poultry. Strawing down – stock now indoors.	From about 11th, tupping (mating). Chest harness containing 'raddle' (colour dye), to mark rumps of mated ewes, is too heavy for rams. Better way of telling if ram has done his duty – if you find him lying down, chewing his cud, he has.	All cattle inside by start of the month, and all dosed for worms. Feed cattle silage and meal. Scrape yards.	Fencing.
Finish ploughing and cultivating. Deliver sugar beet to factory. Maintenance work in workshop. Train employees.	Attending to winter housed stock, turkeys, chickens.	Cull all 'bad doers' – ewes which have not regained healthy body condition necessary to face the winter.	Mainly cattle feeding. Some machinery repairs.	Feeding sheep.

CHAPTER 4

CHANGE IN THE COUNTRYSIDE

There has always been change in the countryside and there always will be. Underlying all the changes brought about by man in his ten-thousand-year tenancy of Britain are the slow processes of change wrought by nature, independent of his influence. You can see them at work in every corner of the countryside, from the seasons' revolving cycle of change throughout the year to the gradual take-over of a disused railway line or section of by-passed road by plants, trees, birds and animals. The longest-lasting and most thorough recording of these natural changes has been unfolding for more than a century at the Rothamsted Experimental Station in Hertfordshire.

The agricultural research station on the Rothamsted estate was founded in 1843 by its owner, John Lawes, who, together with his partner, Henry Gilbert, ran the station for almost sixty years. Lawes was in business as a producer of fertilisers and most of the work at Rothamsted was involved with long-term testing of his products. But he also initiated an experiment on one of his fields, the 10-acre (4-ha) Broadbalk, to see what would happen if nature was allowed its own unimpeded way with a piece of ground. *Guide to the Classical Field Experiments*, which was produced in 1984 by the Rothamsted Experimental Station, puts the results succinctly:

> In 1882 about 0.2 hectares of the wheat crop on land unmanured for many years was enclosed by a fence at the end of the Broadbalk Field nearest the present farm buildings, left unharvested and the land not cultivated. The wheat was left to compete with the weeds and after only four years the few plants surviving were stunted and barely recognizable as cultivated wheat. One half of the area has remained untouched; it is now woodland of mature trees about 20m high, and leading species are ash, sycamore and oak. Hawthorn, now the understorey, is dying out. The ground is covered with ivy in the densest shade, and with dog's mercury, violet and blackberry in the lighter places.
>
> The other half has been cleared of bushes to allow the open-ground vegetation to develop. This consists mainly of coarse grasses, hogweed, agrimony, willow-herb, nettles, knapweed and cow parsley, with many other species in smaller numbers. The bushes that appear are mostly hawthorn, dog-rose, wild plum, blackberry, with a few maple and oak.

CLIMATE
Natural changes, if left alone to operate on the countryside as in that

long-term experiment, will have their own subtle and gradual effects with no help or hindrance from man. But nature in its turn is dependent for the kinds of changes it brings about on the climate in which it is operating. Every aspect of the landscape is influenced in one way or another by the climate and the weather which it produces – natural forces taken to be entirely beyond man's interference from earliest times until our present-day concern with the global warming phenomenon that we seem to have brought on ourselves. Whether the freezing cold of the polar regions, the baking heat of deserts or the moderate, temperate situation that we in Britain enjoy, climate is determined by many delicately balanced factors – the seas and their movements and capacity to absorb or give off heat; the energy poured out by the sun; the atmosphere in a belt around the world that admits and expels rays and gases; the very shape and position of the earth itself.

The climate of any area dictates the amount of rainfall of that region, which helps to shape the landscape through erosion and determines the way its surface cover looks. The naturally mild and wet climate of Britain rounds off the sharp edges of most of our landscape and clothes it in green. The trees, flowers, grasses and crops which are so familiar to us are those best adapted to our cool, humid climate where plenty of rain falls in the spring and autumn, frost and snow bite hard in the winter, and summer brings enough sun to encourage the plants, if not the holidaymaker.

Within this general picture, however, variations are felt from time to time down the centuries as the climate goes temporarily out of balance. For example, towards the end of the sixteenth and seventeenth centuries there was a drop in average temperature of perhaps two or three degrees Centigrade overall. Yet that minor difference produced big changes in the countryside. The winters were reminiscent of the Ice Age. Ferocious gales blew along the coasts – the worst in 1763 killed eight thousand people. Rivers froze for months at a time, birds fell dead in mid-flight, snow-drifts covered much of the country and blocked all roads, bringing normal life to a standstill. For many years of the seventeenth century there was very little rainfall. The Breckland area of Norfolk became a sandy, stony desert where sandstorms blew up. During one, the village of Santon Downham was covered and destroyed.

East Anglia still has one of the lowest averages of rainfall in Britain – about 30in (75cm), roughly four times that of the seventeenth-century droughts. A recent general warming of the earth's climate accounts for the increase – on the west side of Britain, twice that amount of rain falls, especially in the mountain areas of Scotland and Wales. So it is not surprising to find a green lushness in the lowland areas of the West where trees and grass can get a foothold, or to see the warmth-loving corn so vigorous on the rich soils of drier East Anglia.

Wind, too, has its effect on the appearance of the countryside. In the face of salty on-shore winds that have blown unimpeded across the Atlantic for 3,000 miles (4,800km), the mountains and islands of the west coast are virtually treeless, their plants low-lying and their few hardy trees growing short, thick and strong with foliage that is forced into an inland-pointing cluster. In the milder, calmer middle of the country, the great oaks and beeches have the chance to grow to their majestic fullness and height.

A bigger change than man has yet seen in the countryside may shortly occur with the advent of global warming. Nothing has been positively proven yet, but the theory says that our over-production of carbon dioxide through the burning of fossil fuels and the rain forests is absorbing heat from the sun which in the past has always

Caravans line the beach at Mevagissey in Cornwall.

rebounded into space from our atmosphere, and is also blocking the infra-red radiation by which the earth gets rid of the heat which does get through. Some signs of change are already showing themselves in the British climate. The 1980s were the warmest years since records began. Summer droughts and winter storms became commonplace. Springs arrived a month earlier than usual. Something was unsettling the weather. It could just be one of those natural variations to which the world's climate has always been susceptible. But evidence seems to be piling up the other way. Unless we drastically alter our habits, the world may well see an increase in average temperature of about 5.4°F (3°C) by the end of the next century.

When you consider the drastic effects of that average fall of only 3.6°F (2°C) three centuries ago, such a rise could well bring about tremendous changes in the British countryside – the extinction of some cool-climate plants, animals and insects; the appearance of others more tolerant of heat; the south coast basking in dry Mediterranean heat; increased rainfall bringing tropical lushness to the Midlands. And this takes no account of the potential melting of the polar ice-caps, the rise in sea levels and the drowning of many low-lying areas of the world, including a good deal of the east coast of Britain. For once, however, world leaders and their governments, however slowly and patchily, are beginning to make common cause against this threat.

THE POPULAR COUNTRYSIDE

However dramatic the effects of global warming may be on the British landscape, they have still to make any significant impact. There have been plenty of other changes in recent years, however, wrought not by nature but by man. As we have seen, throughout his existence man has changed the surroundings in which he lives as no other animal has done. Change and man are eternal bedfellows. In the twentieth century, the sheer power and influence of his technology have enabled him to stamp his mark all over the countryside. With motor-car, aeroplane and helicopter people can glide like birds from mountain places where only birds have glided before; they can climb rock faces thought unconquerable by their predecessors; they can burrow deep into limestone caves.

And if these remotest and most difficult of places have been conquered and tamed by the well-equipped and determined few, in the rest of the countryside the many have multiplied as never before. Today's town-dwellers think of access to the countryside, to its fields, woods, hills and shores, as a right, rather than as the hard-won and often-withheld privilege it used to be. Gone are the days when ramblers from the northern manufacturing towns had to break out on to the privately owned moors in acts of mass trespassing as they did in the 1930s, to risk a beating from gamekeepers and a spell of imprisonment in order to stake their claim to exercise and recreation in the fresh air. Now people flock to the country in larger

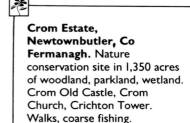

Crom Estate, Newtownbutler, Co Fermanagh. Nature conservation site in 1,350 acres of woodland, parkland, wetland. Crom Old Castle, Crom Church, Crichton Tower. Walks, coarse fishing.

Glen River YMCA National Centre, 143 Central Promenade, Newcastle, Co Down. Canoeing, archery, rock-climbing, camping, orienteering, grass-skiing, hiking in Mourne Mountains. Accommodation in tents (summer) and inside (rest of the year).

Northern Ireland Mountain Centre, Tollymore, Newcastle, Co Down. Mountaineering, rock climbing, canoeing, orienteering, training of mountain leaders.

Sacrewell Farm and Country Centre, Sacrewell, Thornhaugh, Peterborough, Cambridgeshire. Working 500-acre (200ha) farm with trails and guided tours; conservation hand-in-hand with profitable modern farming. Also working water-mill, collection of traditional farm and domestic machines and tools, country crafts and trades, gardens.

New Road Farm, East Huntspill, Somerset. Working 65-acre (26ha) mixed farm: variety of farm and wild animals, children's activity areas, Visitor Centre with interpretive display and collection of rural and farming items. Nature trails. Milking, shearing, feeding, haymaking, farrowing and other farm work.

Stubbs Farm, Kingsley, Bordon, Hampshire. Farm Trail, woodland walk, conservation lakes, farming display.

Rhos-ddu Farm, Crymych, Cardigan, Dyfed, Wales. Working farm with nature trail. Children help feed farm animals and milk cows. Supervised days of activities for children of five-plus.

numbers than ever before, to go fishing, rambling, riding, bicycling, camping, pony-trekking, rock climbing, boating, diving, canoeing, bird watching – or just to have a nice drive and to park their car facing a pleasant view.

Car ownership has been the chief cause of this new freedom, the more so since both country railway and country bus services have been axed or pruned. Shorter working weeks, longer holidays and bigger incomes have also encouraged people to visit the countryside on day trips and weekend excursions. These visitors have brought employment and money into those areas capable of sustaining a tourist industry. But they have also threatened with their sheer weight of numbers to spoil what they value most in those green and pleasant acres – peace and quiet, and absence of other people.

The main problem is that there are simply too many people in too little available countryside. The remoter parts of Britain – the moors, mountains and marshes – have stayed relatively uncrowded, difficult of access and free of facilities as they are. But that puts even greater pressure on those easily accessible, undemanding areas near the big towns. They see too many people in the school holidays and at weekends, their roads clog with cars, their beaches become foul with sewage and plastic, their crops are trampled and fences broken. Some farmers and landowners can be their own worst enemies as far as the country-going public is concerned. Many farmers allow their footpaths to become overgrown and their signposts to fall down, or they sow their crops across the path so that its line is indistinct, and they block their stiles with barbed wire; then they grumble when visiting ramblers stray through corn and hedges trying to find their way. But the visitors keep coming. Both country-dweller and visitor have to try to adapt to each other, and here education plays a vital role. Educating the public can happen with children in the classroom or out in the open; with adults in a purpose-built visitor centre or in chatting across a hedge.

The use of footpaths, the closing of gates, the control of dogs, and so on, are not as self-evident to some visitors as they are to the countryman – sometimes they need to be learned. And farmers do not have to consider it an intrusion when members of the public walk across their private property. With a shift of attitude, footpaths can be seen for what they should be – safe and efficient channels that keep the walkers out of the corn and away from the sheep. In the end, conservation of the countryside is not a matter of controls that are imposed by law, but of individual responsibility learned through experience.

The long-distance footpaths of Britain – the Pennine Way in particular – are beginning to suffer from erosion and from the trampling of surrounding country, simply through over-use by too many ramblers. And these trackways through high and lonely country lose a large part of their appeal if people visiting them can never enjoy a view free of the sight of other ramblers. There is the noise factor, too: it takes only one human voice guffawing or shouting to spoil the solitude of a wild place. But at least a rambler can walk away from all that and find complete peace and silence in the remotest areas of Britain.

Other leisure activities of the country-going public have made more permanent and visible changes to the countryside. The miles of caravans parked along the Norfolk and Lincolnshire cliffs and shores do nothing for the landscape. Neither do the extremely popular theme parks with their many acres of fairground rides, adventure playgrounds and fast-food vans.

COUNTRY CRAFTS

Some changes have been to the benefit of both country-dweller and visitor, and the landscape they both want to enjoy – for example, 'open farms', with animals, nature trails, exhibitions of farming past and present, country crafts and so on, which have revitalised many a run-down farm on the edge of bankruptcy. Open-air museums give visitors first-hand experience of the life of the country and a good walk into the bargain. Such museums are often the best places to see the old-fashioned country crafts being practised.

Until a few years ago, rural skills seemed to be fading slowly away. As life in the countryside changed in response to the demands of the twentieth century, so the making and mending activities that were part of the rural scene – in many cases virtually unchanged since Norman times or before – either died out or fell into decline. Withy-weaving, making pottery by hand, traditional milling by water and wind power, weaving and spinning by hand, thatching, blacksmith and wheelwright work, drystone walling – these and many more rural crafts were conspicuous only by their absence, or by the overgrown withy beds, derelict mills and tumbledown stone walls to be seen in the landscape.

A revival of interest in country crafts has occurred for two main reasons: there has been a reawakening of interest in conservation and in using one's own hands and simple, traditional tools, and the last decade has seen the emergence of the rural museums. It might be argued that the best way to see country crafts in action is as they are naturally practised in the normal course of country life. Certainly, there is an added pleasure in watching a hedge being laid in the traditional fashion on a working farm by a farmer doing it that way because he prefers it that way. But if one is in the middle of a large tract of countryside in which all the farmers use hedge-rippers, it is good to know that the local rural life museum is managing its hedgerows traditionally. There it is an artificial craft, in one sense, but the wildlife that gathers under such a hedge's protection is real enough.

One can divide the present practice of country crafts and industries in Britain into three main types: those that are practised

Blackshaw Farm Park, near West Kilbride, Strathclyde, Scotland. Working farm; sheep dipping and shearing, milking cows, feeding calves. Nature trails, tractor-and-trailer rides, grass sledging, four-wheel motorbikes.

Blowplain Open Farm, Balmaclellan, Castle Douglas, Dumfries and Galloway, Scotland. Guided tour around day-to-day life of small Scottish hill farm, featuring different types of animals and their uses.

Folly Farm, Begelly, Kilgetty, Pembrokeshire, Dyfed, South-West Wales. Working dairy farm. Viewing of machine-milking; try hand milking. Museum of bygone dairying equipment. Other farm animals; play area; tea room with home-made specialities; nature trail; tractor and trailer rides.

The Crafts Study Centre, Holburne of Menstrie Museum, Great Pulteney Street, Bath, Avon. Archive, collections and exhibitions of twentieth-century British crafts: ceramics, printed and woven textiles, calligraphy, furniture making.

Ewenny Pottery, Bridgend, Mid-Glamorgan, Wales. Pottery founded in eighteenth-century and still in same family. Everyone welcome to watch the potter at work.

Mill Green Water Mill, Mill Green, Hatfield, Hertfordshire. Mill on Domesday site; rebuilt c1762 and 1824, abandoned 1911, renovated 1973 onwards, recommenced milling flour 1986. Visitors can view milling and buy flour. Local history museum in miller's house next door, from Roman times to present day. Craft displays and demonstrations in summer.

Chaff cutters and mangold slicers at Sacrewell Farm and Country Centre.

(Below left) Celt outside his Iron Age house at the Chiltern Open Air Museum.

(Below right, and Opposite above) Iron Age Celt and nuclear age children meet across 2,000 years.

(Below) Harrowing the medieval fields at the Chiltern Open Air Museum.

John Webb's Windmill, Thaxted, Essex. Tower mill built 1804, disused by 1910, restored 1973 onwards. Intention to mill flour again one day. Museum of local items on ground floor.

Quantock Weavers, The Old Forge, Plainsfield, Over Stowey, Bridgwater, Somerset. Housed in seventeenth-century barn turned blacksmith's forge turned spinners' workshop. Courses and demonstrations of spinning and weaving. Hand-knitted garments, and hand-woven rugs and wall coverings, in hand-spun and natural-dyed wool.

Amberley Chalk Pits Museum, Amberley, near Arundel, West Sussex. Working blacksmith among other rural craft workers: wheelwright, potter, brickmaker. Photographic display of past chalk working activities on the site. Original kilns still in place, where chalk was burned to make lime for spreading on heavy or poor soils. Also narrow-gauge railway, industrial buildings, tools, machines.

Ballycopeland Windmill, near Millisle, Co Down. Eighteenth-century tower mill, the only working windmill in Ireland. Wooden mill machinery, old milling tools on display. Visitor centre; hands-on experience of milling.

Ardess Craft Centre, Ardess House, Kesh, Co Fermanagh. Residential craft centre in renovated Georgian rectory. Spinning and weaving tuition; also appliqué, basket weaving, painting, tapestry weaving, machine knitting, natural dyeing, screen printing, furniture restoring, courses on botany and geology. Craft shop.

as livelihoods or methods of maintenance with no reliance on or courting of visitors; those which, while they are proper commercial enterprises, are glad of outside interest and money, and make some effort to attract visitors; and those that are practised entirely under artificial conditions, such as in a rural life museum, on which they rely for their existence.

The first category embraces such activities as drystone walling, thatching, peat cutting and cider-making – work that continues in all weathers, in solitude or under an onlooker's gaze. Farmers in drystone wall areas such as the northern fells and the Cotswolds still bemoan the passing of the skill; barbed wire is cheaper and easier. Drystone walling, like hedge-laying, has nothing except interest to offer the visitor. There are no end results to buy; no money comes the craftsman's way from his onlookers.

The thatcher, on the other hand, gets paid for his skill. Thatching is a reviving craft; not only because a thatched roof is satisfying to look at, but because, with rising heating costs, the virtue of thatch as an efficient and long-lasting insulation material is being appreciated anew.

Some peat-cutting concerns are organised on a huge commercial scale, with machines scooping up tons of peat for back gardens or whisky distilleries; some combine machine-cutting and hand-cutting, and provide a display for visitors; some peat is entirely hand-cut to provide fuel for the cutter himself – this practice is almost exclusive to rural Ireland and the Scottish Highlands and islands. And as for cider-making, one only has to enter the cool, fragrant depths of a cider shed in Somerset or Herefordshire, and see the customers with their gallon containers slowly sampling the various blends, to realise that this particular delightful rural industry-cum-pleasure will continue for ever.

A rural craft such as the weaving of baskets from Somerset withies or willow wands might well disappear without the support of visitors' money. Watching the whippy wands rattling through the stripping machine and then being bent and woven into shape is fascinating, and buying a sample of what you have just seen in creation is satisfying. Probably a few people in the Somerset Levels would go on making withy baskets in their back rooms for their own satisfaction, even if the visitors never came to see and buy; but the little shops, the explanatory leaflets and the trails to the withy beds have kept a handful of local basket-makers from going out of business.

The numerous potteries that have sprung up in villages all over the country in recent years, and the weavers and spinners who set up their looms and wheels in converted schoolhouses and cowsheds, old barns and forges, have also been supported by tourism. The decline of these activities from cottage industry to enthusiast's hobby has been halted, if not reversed, by the ability of their practitioners to accommodate and benefit from the interest of visiting outsiders in what they make and how they make it.

Miller's waggon before
restoration . . .

. . . and after restoration at
Avoncroft Museum, Worcestershire.

Tregwynt Woollen Mill, near St Nicholas, Letterston, Haverfordwest, Dyfed, Wales. Old mill ½ mile (0.8km) from lovely beaches. Visitors watch weaving in the mill and buy products.

Ruskin Mill, Nailsworth, Stroud, Gloucestershire. Old textile mill, renovated by voluntary labour and housing craft workshops. Public welcome to see all activities: leather, glass and metal workers, potters, artists, boat-builder.

The Willows Peat Company, Shapwick Road, Westhay, near Glastonbury, Somerset. Peat Moors Visitor Centre: commercial peat operation and garden centre, but visitors catered for with demonstrations and have-a-go sessions of hand-cutting with traditional tools and building cut peats into a 'hyle' or aerated structure. Display of the story of peat and peat-cutting in the Somerset Levels.

Dunkerton's Cider Company, Hays Road, Luntley, Pembridge, Leominster, Herefordshire. Varieties of cider and perry made – watch the process, then drink the product! No chemical sprays used on apples; no colouring, flavouring or preservatives added to ciders or perry. Rare cider apple orchards planted to preserve apples that might otherwise die out.

P. Coate & Son, Meare Green Court, Stoke St Gregory, Taunton, Somerset. Family basket-makers. Guided Willow Trail through process: sorting withies (willow wands), boiling, stripping, drying, tying, basket-making. Waymarked walk to the withy beds. Showroom and wetland exhibition. Museum.

The rural museums, of course, rely entirely on visitor interest for their survival, along with any grants they may receive. The black-smiths and wheelwrights, the furniture makers and woodworkers who operate in these sheltered conditions are protected from the icy breath of the marketplace as craftsmen in the other categories are not – although they do depend on the overall success of the museum, of course. But their skills are preserved and are seen in operation by thousands of people, as they might not be in the harsh and realistic world outside. You can still find a working blacksmith or two outside the confines of a rural museum, probably earning a living by repairing farm machinery and making tools as well as fancy ironwork for the luxury or tourist trade. But smaller, special-ist practitioners of country crafts – the makers of corn dollies, lace

Laying a hedge in the old traditional way.

142

Thatching – a country craft that has
never died out.

Kersey Pottery, The Street, Kersey, Suffolk. Housed in buildings of old River House Farm by the watersplash. Stoneware pottery decorated with original glazes and distinctive patterns; all processes open to public.

Wirral Country Park, Station Road, Thurstaston, Wirral. 12-mile (19-km) linear country park laid out along disused railway line. Planned with potential clients from nearby Merseyside in mind. Visitor Centre with displays of local geology, history and wildlife; story of railway and creation of country park. Hadlow Road Station display – a country station in 1952.

and rag rugs, the spinners of rabbit wool and hand-churners of butter – are as grateful to the rural museums for space, facilities and an audience as the museums are to them for offering their talents and skills.

RURAL HARMONY

Some country parks have been designed specifically for use by town-dwellers – for example, the Wirral Country Park near Birkenhead and Liverpool, based on a disused railway line, which was set up by Cheshire County Council in the 1970s to provide rural recreation for urban people, as was the Lea Valley recreational area that leads from east London into Hertfordshire. In fact, the recreation officers of the county and borough councils are important people these days; no longer just token figures, they work closely with planners and local conservation and wildlife bodies to smooth the path of the town into the country and to find ways of fitting the quart of the public into the pint pot of the countryside.

If relations between farmers and the country-going public are often strained, the relationship between the farmer and the land – the farmer and his neighbouring wildlife – must be at an all-time low. The development of chemical pesticides, herbicides, fungicides and fertilisers has brought about an explosion in crop production since World War II. It seems that farmers, spurred on by grants and EC directives, are unable to stop producing food, even if the produce ends up poured into milk lakes or piled into mountains of grain, butter or meat. Meanwhile, the butterflies, birds, insects, flowers and small animals of the hedgerows, cornfields and pastures fall in their millions to the cocktail of killing poisons that frees the crops from insects and diseases.

Many chemicals have been banned as their disastrous effect on wildlife has become clear – for example, the organochlorines such as DDT, dieldrin, aldrin and endrin. The soil becomes exhausted through over-stimulation by the nitrates of artificial fertilisers, which are washed by rain into the nearby ditches, ponds, streams and rivers, as well as into lakes and reservoirs. These nitrates can cause havoc in the watercourses of the countryside.

It would be wrong to think that all farmers are greedy, uncaring polluters and destroyers. The conservation work of Bob Peters, John and Rosemary Berry, Jerry Harding and the other farmers described in Chapter 3 shows what can be done if agricultural producers are prepared to replant hedges, cut down or abandon altogether the use of chemicals, leave areas of untouched ground for wildlife, clean up their spillages and in general face up to their responsibilities in the countryside. But the example of the effects of nitrate pollution on a river serves as a chilling illustration of how closely enmeshed the parts of nature are, and how vulnerable they are to human carelessness.

When a river is unaffected by human interference, it is a teeming, balanced, interdependent storehouse of wildlife. Fish, water creatures, plants and microscopic organisms all live in its waters. Insects hover over it. Reeds, trees and wild flowers grow on its banks. This combination of food and shelter brings dragonflies to hunt the insects, small birds to hunt the dragonflies and hawks to hunt the small birds. If the area is fortunate, otters may come to hunt the fish. In the bankside vegetation nest reed warblers and reed buntings, coots and moorhens. Deer, foxes, badgers, rabbits, stoats, snakes and every other kind of creature come to drink from the river. It is the centre of life for a diverse animal and plant community.

If an area becomes polluted, this delicate balance is entirely upset. The most direct kind of pollution, the spillage of poison into the water, may kill everything simply by ingestion through drinking or by direct poisoning. But such spillages are rare. A much more common case is pollution through nitrate-sodden run-off from adjacent farm fields. This kind of everyday occurrence sets off a chain reaction that reaches every corner of animal life in, above and near the river. Algae thrive in the nitrate-enriched water, blocking out sunlight and gobbling up oxygen. Plants die in the murky, soupy water from lack of oxygen and sun. Fish and other water creatures die from lack of plant food, or leave that particular stretch of the river. The kingfishers, dippers, swallows and herons, the dragonflies and otters, finding nothing to eat, abandon the river as well.

As the plants along the bank die off, so the bank itself begins to crumble, with no plant roots to hold it together. Water rats leave their collapsed holes. The trees lose their root grip in the shaky bank soil and fall or wither. With the fall of the trees, whole colonies of fungi, lichens and insects disappear, and so do the tree-nesting birds. The reed warbler and reed bunting are seen no more. The harriers, kestrels and sparrowhawks find no small birds and they, too, quit the now lifeless river. This scene is rarely played out to such a grim end in actuality, since amounts of nitrates getting into a river vary enormously from month to month and river water renews itself every second as it passes by. But certainly there are many sterile, fishless, birdless and all but plantless rivers in the most intensely cultivated and fertilised corn- and vegetable-growing areas of eastern England. And three out of four of the Norfolk Broads, those old flooded peat-diggings with water either static or only very slowly moving, are barren algal soups.

Farm pollution often brings about destructive change in the countryside in these gradual and occasionally hard-to-notice ways. The effects of industry in changing the countryside, on the other hand, have been brutally and glaringly obvious since steam and the Industrial Revolution first teamed up, and things have not altered for the better. Mining and quarrying provide raw materials we would not like to be without – not just coal and stone, but china clay, sand, chalk, gravel, clay for bricks and ore for smelting. But they also create deserts of ugliness with their pits and holes, heaps and wastes – black, white or grey land from which the life departs with

(Above, below, opposite above)
Peat cutting on the Somerset Levels
at the turn of the century . . .

(Below) . . . and as it still is in the Isle of Skye.

the colour. Of Britain's 50 million acres (20 million ha), probably a quarter of a million (100,000ha) are derelict industrial land which needs massive and radical treatment to put it back into any sort of use: abandoned coal mines and tips in Scotland, the North-East, Yorkshire, Nottinghamshire, South Wales; derelict brickfields in Bedfordshire and pottery clay holes in Staffordshire; waste heaps and disused shafts of lead mines in the Yorkshire Dales, ironstone mines in the Midlands, tin mines in Cornwall, gashes and scars of quarries in the Mendip Hills – the list goes on.

These derelict places, ugly as they look, lie inert. But industry can have harmful effects on the countryside of a much more lively kind, with toxic dumps, leakage of chemicals, pollutants and radio-active materials from toxic dumps, badly maintained sewage farms, carelessly run factories and power plants; sulphur-laden acid rain defoliating forests and sterilising lakes in Scotland; chemical works emitting lung-searing and eye-stinging 'quite harmless' vapours from the chimneys.

How far industrial pollution has gone in damaging the country-side is hard to assess, since at the same time strenuous efforts are being made to clear up and reclaim as much derelict land as possible. Many extraction industries – for example, ironstone workings and stone quarries – are required by law these days to restore the land once they have finished with it. This can involve land-scaping the rough edges, infilling, turfing over, planting trees and perhaps flooding a pit to make an artificial lake.

Many of the valleys of South Wales have exchanged their old black coats for new green ones since the colliery wheels stopped turning and the smelting furnaces went cold. Grimy feeder ponds for ironworks have become landscaped lakes; enormous barren slagheaps now resemble grassy hills; devastated areas of former coal mines have been converted into parks and play areas. These are admirable schemes.

Waste from many sources can be used to restore derelict land – for example, power station coal cinders can be used to fill in brickfields, or a town's rubbish can infill a disused mineshaft. Old gravel pits near Cirencester have been converted into the Cotswold Water Park. The city of Stoke-on-Trent, with its clay extraction pits, collieries and maze of industrial railway lines, had in the 1960s more derelict land than any other local authority in Britain; now-adays, there are sports grounds, parks and footpaths where desola-tion once ruled.

The Lower Swansea Valley, which was crowded with processing plants for steel, coal, tin, zinc and copper, was so blighted by poison-ous fumes and waste at the turn of this century that no plants sur-vived on the steep valley sides, whose naked topsoil was washed away by rainfall to produce a bare desert landscape. A report on the devastation, published in the 1960s, was the catalyst for a programme of reclamation which is still under way and which has seen wildlife beginning to find its place again in the landscape.

Chwarel Wynne Slate Mine and Museum, Glyn Ceiriog, near Llangollen, Clwyd, Wales. Guided tours around floodlit underground slate workings. Museum with display on work and domestic life of Victorian slate-mining village.

Cwm-Celyn Lake, Blaina, near Abertillery, Gwent, South Wales. Nineteenth-century feeder pond for Blaina ironworks, now landscaped walking and picnicking area. Fishing available.

Rhondda Heritage Park, Trehafod, near Pontypridd, Mid-Glamorgan, South Wales. Heritage and industrial project showing life in the valleys through the centuries. Visitor Centre; exhibitions.

Swansea Maritime and Industrial Museum, Museum Square, Maritime Quarter, Swansea, West Glamorgan, Wales. Displays, photographs, maps, items from Lower Swansea Valley's industrial past – Swansea was known in Victorian days as 'Copperopolis'. Also relics of Swansea's ships that imported copper ore, and much else from the town's industrial, maritime and social history.

These are only a few examples of reclamation schemes, which are often carried out with the help of local schoolchildren and other volunteer working parties. Other sites have been restored and opened to the public as working exhibitions of their industrial past – collieries, mills, slate mines, railway centres, ironworks.

Industries which have now declined are mostly responsible for the kind of destruction of the countryside outlined above. Those making the enormous effort to restore landscape that has been damaged by industry can at least be confident that nothing similar is likely to rear its head in their area again. What saps that confidence and threatens the will to tackle such tasks is the recent encroachment on the countryside of developments on the outskirts of towns – business parks, enormous new amusement and theme parks and housing developments – and the building of hundreds of miles of new roads, which cut through irreplaceable wetlands, downs and farmland with economic expansion as their justification. It is hard to argue against the creation of new jobs and fresh injections of money, especially when the objectors cannot point to belching chimneys, mountainous slagheaps or miles of derelict ground to support their case. And where big business leads, protected by all its advantages of funds, influence and governmental backing, the greedy and selfish small operator can follow. These small acts of vandalism, which are often reported only in the local press, are in their way more disheartening than the corporate swallowing-up of the countryside.

What safeguards can be effective against – to take a few recent instances – the Norfolk farmer who ploughs a large V-sign across his marshes in defiance of a campaign by local conservationists; or the thief who robs an osprey's nest in Scotland to sell the eggs for thousands of pounds to a collector from the Middle East; or the Welsh farmer who puts out poisoned bait for the red kites that have just been released to breed in his valley; or the Essex landowner who sprays a field of rare orchids with herbicides at the dead of night to remove the obstacle to his housing scheme; or the Birmingham developer who brings in his bulldozer early one Sunday morning when no one is about, to knock down an Elizabethan country house with a preservation order on it which the city council and the entire local community wants to save from demolition? 'Once it's done, it's done – so I'll do it if I want to,' is the attitude of such people. Eternal vigilance is the only way to thwart such destruction. But nothing seems to be truly effective against these individual acts of bloody-minded selfishness.

VILLAGE LIFE

Some of the biggest changes of recent years have taken place literally on the countryman's doorstep – in the village where he lives. The romantic image of the village is of thatched cottages clustering around the village green and duckpond, the church tower peeping

Gloddfa Ganol Slate Mine, Blaenau Ffestiniog, Gwynedd, North Wales. The largest slate mine in the world, open for trips, slate railway rides, exhibitions of the mine's working past. Slate mill in operation; shops; restaurant; exhibition hall; trail through huge underground caverns blasted out by slate miners.

Llechwedd Slate Caverns, Blaenau Ffestiniog, Gwynedd, North Wales. Huge underground chambers, exhibitions, display of life of a Victorian miner. Miners' tramway train ride through caverns with mining tableaux; deep mine trip by Britain's steepest passenger incline railway. Miners Arms pub.

Blaenafon Ironworks, Blaenafon, Gwent, South Wales. Eighteenth-century ironworks – guided tours around the remains of blast furnaces, casting houses and ironworkers' dwellings.

Big Pit, Blaenafon, Gwent, South Wales. Big Pit mine closed 1980; underground tours by tramway of the workings. Winding engine house, blacksmith's shop, pithead baths. Exhibitions.

Loch Garten Nature Reserve, near Aviemore, Highland, Scotland. Observation hut with binoculars for viewing osprey nest in treetop; ospreys returned to breed here in 1959 after years of absence from Scotland. Loch and forest wildlife and walks nearby.

Cutting the withy beds.

Ulster Folk and Transport Museum, Cultra Manor, Holywood, Co Down.
Buildings re-erected on site include terraces, parish church, schoolhouse, flax scutching mill, farmhouses, spade mill, cottiers' houses, forge. Transport collection features donkey carts, bicycles, aircraft, merchant schooner, cars, miniature railway. Exhibitions of country and domestic crafts, ploughing, harvesting, threshing. Farm animals.

Tying withy bundles at Coate's in Somerset before World War I.

Tying withies today.

Avoncroft Museum of Buildings, Stoke Heath, Bromsgrove, Worcestershire. Open air museum with more than twenty buildings, from early medieval times to present day; all saved from demolition, dismantled and re-erected at Avoncroft. Includes fourteenth-century roof of priory guest hall, fifteenth-century and Tudor merchants' houses, a Georgian cockpit, a Victorian chainshop from the Black Country and a 1940s prefab. Demonstrations and practical application of traditional building skills as well as modern ones. Shire horse gives waggon rides.

Ryedale Folk Museum, Hutton-le-Hole, York. Local cruck house, cottage, manor house re-erected at museum; also new sheds, barns and traditional-style crofter's cottage. Craft workshops and displays include blacksmith, shoemaker, tinsmith, cooper, cabinetmaker, chemist, small iron foundry, saddler, wheelwright, thatching, lace-making, turf-cutting.

Weald and Downland Open Air Museum, Singleton, near Chichester, West Sussex. Many local buildings saved from demolition and rebuilt at museum: medieval houses, water-mill, Tudor market hall, village school, barns. Woodland walk through this 40-acre (16ha) site.

Basket making at Coate's.

Restoring the land; Bonds Yard nr
Chesterfield before restoration . . .   . . . and after.

Pemberton Site nr Wigan before
restoration . . .   . . . and after.

Ramcroft Site before restoration . . .

. . . and after.

Individual acts of selfishness –
rubbish dumping on Southwick
Marsh SSSI.

Cottage thatch and cottage garden,
the romantic ideal of village England.

over the trees, winding lanes leading to mellow old farmhouses and their chicken-clucking yards surrounded by great barns crammed with the produce of the farm. Somewhere in the picture is the village pub with its nut-brown ale and gossiping farmhands, the squire and vicar in their fine houses, the sun shining over maypole dancers on the green. For generations this seductive ideal has been a powerful magnet for outsiders, who hope to find in the village the settled way of life, the sense of order and peace that is lacking in the towns and cities to which they belong. Day visitors to the villages of Britain's countryside probably get closest to that dream – they can arrive by car, train or bus, wander around in a daze of delight and go home in the evening with a camera full of enchanting memories and all their illusions still intact. A more powerful force for change in the village, however, is exerted by those who most wish for things to stay unchanged – the retired folk, the commuters, the weekenders and the escapers from city life who come to set up home and stay.

'Oh, my son couldn't afford to buy a house here, and there aren't the jobs like there used to be. He had to go off to Norwich when he got married,' said the old villager to me, standing at the door of his council house on the outskirts of the Norfolk farming village. He had been a thatcher until the 1960s when demand for his skills had been killed off by the arrival of modern synthetic roofing materials. A bundle of rusty old thatching hooks lay on the shelf in his garden shed. 'You can have that, if you want,' the old man muttered, holding out a handful of hooks, 'they're no good to me any more.' The cottage where he was born (and his father and grandfather), renamed 'Thatchers', was now the property of a solicitor from London who came down with his family twice a month in the summer to spend the weekend. 'Never see them in the pub, nor the shop. Bring all their own food and drink with them, you see. And of course we never see them at all in the winter – maybe at the New Year. And they're not the only ones. The centre of this village is mostly dead then, most of those old cottages empty. It's a shame.'

That village on the North Norfolk coast was lucky in one way – neither of the two farmers who still held land thereabouts had yet sold their fields to developers. The growth of new housing developments, sprouting dreams of 'desirable residences' on decommissioned farmland, has swelled enormously in the last couple of decades. It is rare to find one of these new instant villages built in a style that harmonises with its long-established neighbour. Too often the designs seem to be taken from some all-purpose builder's pattern-book – twenty new black-tiled roofs next to two old thatched ones, five red-brick houses filling in a gap between two cottages of lichened stone. Such new houses dictate an urban way of living for their inhabitants, clustered together as they would have been in the town. But it is the incomers who buy up the old village houses at inflated prices that locals cannot afford who have brought about the most profound change in the villages.

Mechanised farming has done away with most of the jobs that

local people used to rely on. Nowadays the majority of villages within 50 miles (80km) of London have populations made up chiefly of incomers, almost all commuters who only see their village at night-time and at weekends. To look at, these villages – and others like them, within an hour's driving distance of big towns and cities all over the country – are in better shape than ever they were before the train and the motor-car made commuting possible. The lanes are clear of rubbish, the gardens immaculate, the houses themselves provided with modern services, maintained and cared for in a way the original villagers would never have found time and money for. And, paradoxically, the community spirit of these efficient villages is still strong. You don't buy into a dream without working to make that dream come true. The fêtes, the amateur dramatic clubs and morris dancing sides, the village shows and societies all thrive, supported and maintained largely by the newcomers. Born-and-bred locals may join in, or they may retire to the pub and keep out of the way of the enthusiastic new villagers. Their familiar village may be fast vanishing under the weight of Volvos and black labradors – potent symbols everywhere of the wealthy incomer – but a new and vigorous community of a different sort has already taken root.

Auchindrain Old Highland Township, Inveraray, Strathclyde, Scotland. Ancient communal tenancy township, still on original site in original form, now with buildings restored and furnished as display of traditional Highland life through the ages.

Eco-friendly technology for tomorrow: a turf-roofed constant temperature store at the Centre for Alternative Technology at Machynlleth, North Wales.

Museum of Lakeland Life and Industry, Abbot Hall, Kendal, Cumbria. Displays of working and everyday life in Lake District, both in the past and today. Includes printing, wool spinning and weaving, mining and quarrying, farming, clothing; rural trades and industries such as blacksmiths, wheelwrights and cart-builders. Also interior of Lakeland cottages.

Museum of East Anglian Life, Stowmarket, Suffolk. Collection of horse-drawn vehicles, agricultural tools and machines, craft implements and domestic items, showing daily life and work in old-time East Anglia. Buildings include medieval barn, windpump, eighteenth-century water-mill, smithy, fourteenth-century aisled hall.

Shetland Croft House Museum, Southvoe, Dunrossness, Shetland Mainland. Thatched Shetland croft house, with outbuildings and working water-mill, furnished in style of 1860.

Tingwall Agricultural Museum, Veensgarth, Lerwick, Shetland Mainland. Mid-eighteenth-century granary, stables, bothy and smithy house, tools and equipment used by traditional Shetland crofter, as well as tools of blacksmith, wheelwright and cooper.

Centre for Alternative Technology, Llwyngwern Quarry, Pantperthog, Machynlleth, Powys, Wales. Introductory display. Demonstrations of all kinds of alternative technology; the centre and its inhabitants live by the principles they advocate. Windmills, solar panels, organic gardens, waterwheels, wind turbines, self-build housing, energy conservation, waste recycling, etc. Also woodland walks, maze, adventure playground.

In the countryside beyond the commuter's range, however, the life of many villages that are less galvanised by modern money and aspirations is undergoing a slow strangulation as the vital oxygen of self-sufficiency is gradually cut off. The village school, post office, shop, pub, railway station, bus service; the policeman, the vicar, the gamekeeper and the roadmender: these have disappeared or are disappearing from the remoter villages. It is just not economical to keep them going.

There was certainly nothing particularly romantic about traditional village life in the 'Golden Age' before World War I, with its cramped, damp cottages, its crippling ignorance, its poverty and oppressive social order. But it survived, largely independent of outside money and attention, sustained by the cradle-to-the-grave involvement of all its inhabitants in the work of the countryside in which it was set. Those who still work in this way have a positive part to play in the well-being of the village, as do the incomers who set up their own small-scale businesses, be they potters, musicians, weavers, smallholders, cider-makers, boat-builders, carpenters or curators of local museums. Most of these new villagers do not expect to get rich, many of them having turned their backs on lucrative but unsatisfying jobs.

Putting down roots is all very well, but roots need nourishing. Grants, loans, expert advice and other forms of encouragement and practical help are needed if village life in remote places is to be preserved and if incomers and locals are to value and work with each other. Perhaps these villages, now shorn of most of their services and means of support, will come into their own again when oil and coal eventually run out and we are all obliged to hark back to the basics of life once more.

CHAPTER 5
NATIONAL PARKS AND COUNTRYSIDE ORGANISATIONS

In Chapter 4 we looked briefly at the increasing prominence in the countryside of farm parks, open-air museums and country parks, and their beneficial effects in attracting people to the countryside while at the same time limiting the disruption by keeping all their visitors in one defined area; we also saw their success in safeguarding country crafts and in educating young and old about the countryside and its life.

The desire to be out and about in the countryside is not new. On the contrary – as more people crammed into the towns and cities from the countryside during the Industrial Revolution, many felt more and more keenly the need to escape to the surrounding fields, hills, moors and woods. At the same time the Romantic Movement was influencing people's view of the landscape, opening their eyes to the beauty and excitement of natural shapes, colours and textures in the countryside. With the advent of railway travel, the bicycle, the bus and the private motor-car, allied to a shorter working week and more paid holidays, people felt by the turn of this century that they had a right to roam in the country. But so much of Britain was, and still is, in private hands. The Manchester Ramblers with their historic mass trespasses on to the nearby moors in 1932 were expressing widely felt frustration with landowners who refused point blank to allow any public access at all on to their tens of thousands of acres of open countryside. Some of the Manchester Ramblers went to jail to prove their point, and these confrontations did stir up a great deal of interest in the whole topic.

THE NATIONAL PARKS

After World War II, Britain's network of national parks was set up in response to the general atmosphere of rebuilding and re-evaluation. The 1945 report to the government by John Dower of the Standing Committee on National Parks defined the concept of a national park as an extensive area of beautiful and relatively wild country in which, for the nation's benefit and by appropriate national decision and action,

(a) the characteristic landscape beauty is strictly preserved;
(b) access and facilities for public open-air enjoyment are amply provided;
(c) wildlife and buildings and places of architectural and historic interest are suitably protected; while
(d) established farming use is effectively maintained.

Dove Cottage, Town End, Grasmere, Cumbria. Cottage where the poet William Wordsworth and his sister Dorothy lived, now restored as a museum. Adjacent museum display tells story of Wordsworth's life and his influence in opening eyes and hearts to beauties of landscape.

Bridge Cottage, Flatford, Suffolk. Display tells the story of John Constable and his paintings. 'Constable Country' lies all around, with scenes from many of his best-known landscapes: *Flatford Mill, Boat-building near Flatford Mill, The Valley of the Stour, with Dedham in the Distance, The Haywain, Dedham Lock and Mill.*

Elgar's Birthplace, Crown East Lane, Lower Broadheath, Worcester. Cottage where composer Sir Edward Elgar was born, set in countryside near Malvern Hills that inspired much of his music. Personal memorabilia, family photographs, manuscripts, scores, concert programmes, press cuttings.

The national parks ought to be acknowledged as among Britain's greatest national treasures and resources. We ought to be bursting with pride in the very fact of their existence. Everyone in Britain should be able to reel off the names of the parks and a list of the glories that each contains. Yet I wonder how many of these parks people could name, if asked? The national parks were never mentioned during my schooldays, and they were never discussed later, in conversation at work or in the pub. I knew of the areas in which they lay and had visited many of them, but I was in ignorance of their status and of their day-to-day aims and objectives.

The National Parks Authorities themselves, researching for their 'awareness campaign' in 1987, were appalled to discover how few people had heard of them or their work. Yet as pressure on the countryside increases, it is to the national parks that people will be looking for guidelines and models of how to reconcile the beautiful countryside and its characteristic wildlife, buildings and farming practices with greater and greater numbers of visitors. Demand for open space for rambling and recreation – the 'natural' open space of the kind that a leisure park or a rural museum cannot offer – grows year by year, coming into conflict with the desperate need of wildlife to be left undisturbed in its own habitat. Here the national parks, supposedly secure from free-for-all exploitation and development, have a vital role to play.

In the 1950s the ten national parks came into being: Dartmoor and Exmoor in the south-west of England; the Peak District in the northern Midlands; the Yorkshire Dales and the North York Moors; further north the Lake District and Northumberland; in Wales the Brecon Beacons, the Pembrokeshire Coast and Snowdonia. These were the Magnificent Ten, which were joined in 1989 by the Norfolk and Suffolk Broads (for some technical reason not officially to be labelled a national park). The landscape of Scotland, so much of it far more inaccessible, was not felt at the time of the national park designations to be so vulnerable, and still lies outside the national park umbrella, as does the Northern Irish landscape. The ten national parks and their younger East Anglian associate are not superior in appearance or atmosphere to every other non-designated area of England and Wales, but they do contain within their 5,450 square miles (14,115km²) a large amount of outstandingly beautiful and interesting countryside.

Dartmoor and Exmoor are the two West Country sisters at opposite ends of Devon, entirely unlike each other in character: Dartmoor the dark and Exmoor the fair. Dartmoor's extremes of weather, its mists and rains, are famed and feared by walkers, as are its bogs that can swallow sheep, horses and people, its grim prison at Princetown, its prehistoric hut circles and field systems and its stony tors like totem faces bitten out of the granite by wind and rain. Bleakness is Dartmoor's chief characteristic and also its glory. Here you can feel further away from it all than almost anywhere else in England. Exmoor, by contrast, is a warm-feeling place; it has long rolling shoulders of smooth hill ridge and deep combes or valleys lined with trees where wild red deer hide; buzzards and badgers; *Lorna Doone* and *Tarka the Otter*; and rounded headlands falling to pebbly beaches unvisited by tourists even in the height of summer.

In the North Midlands, the Peak District has a twin nature too, divided as it is between the limestone dales of the White Peak and the peat moorlands of the Dark Peak. They offer a tremendous variety of mood and appearance to the many millions of visitors every year who go for a 'day out in the Peaks' from the big industrial towns and cities of the Midlands and South Yorkshire. In the Peak District you can find scenery as utterly contrasted as the plunging, winding limestone valley of Dovedale with its rock pinnacles and towers, and the black, sodden peat moors around Kinder Scout where the Pennine Way starts. The Yorkshire Dales and the North York Moors are further evidence of the variety found within the national parks, from the lovely limestone dales of Yorkshire's heartland with their remote farms and stone barns to the great cliffs and huddled fishing villages of the North York Moors, the many acres of woodlands and the enormous stretch of the moorlands themselves.

The Lake District is probably the best known of the national parks and the one most under threat from the sheer numbers of visitors who pour in every year to walk the fells, laze or water-sport around the lakes or visit sites connected with William and Dorothy Wordsworth. You can walk away from all the other people and up into heavenly solitude in the remoter hills and valleys, but at holiday seasons the central and southern lakes and their little towns – Keswick, Grasmere, Windermere, Ambleside – are often unpleasantly packed and noisy.

Overcrowding is never a problem in the least-known, most northerly and most remote of the national parks, Northumberland. Some 400 square miles (1,000km²) lie between Hadrian's Wall and the rolling, grassy Cheviot Hills on the Scottish Border, and most of it is entirely empty of humans. Here, as on Dartmoor, you can feel truly alone on hilltop and moor or in the coniferous depths of Wark Forest or Kielder Forest.

The three Welsh parks show the three most celebrated characteristics of Welsh landscape: the craggy coast of cliffs, bays and islands in the Pembrokeshire Coast park, the Brecon Beacons and their blend of steeply scarped fells and small market towns, and Snowdonia with its great mountains and its slate quarries, narrow-gauge steam railways and long sandy estuaries.

Most of the land within the national parks is privately owned, and the parks themselves are each run by a National Park Authority, or NPA, which has to walk a tightrope among the varying demands of local agriculture and forestry, local business, local residents, local and national wildlife and conservation organisations, the visiting public and the ever-eager developers and road-builders waiting for

a loophole to squeeze through. The NPAs' budgets are tight – most of their money comes from central government, with the local county councils putting in a proportion – their obligations daunting and their work-load enormous. They have to keep the landowners as sweet as possible with grants, advice and consultation, and with a little discreet stick or carrot if they feel it is necessary. They have to act as a bridge between public and landowners, between landowners and local government. They are charged with responsibility for footpath upkeep, for information, for signposting, car parks, picnic sites, study centres. They have to see that mineral extraction, forestry and farming, road-building and the provision of such essential public amenity installations as reservoirs, pumping stations and power stations are managed without endangering the landscape and character of their park. They have to try to minimise the noise and disturbance from the military training grounds that are sited in many of the parks – for example, Dartmoor and Northumberland, or the Lake District where the screech of a jet threading a valley at hair-parting height has become a part of the scene.

The ironic feature of the duties entrusted to the National Park Authorities is that they have all these responsibilities and very little power to back them up. If a jet pilot decides to scream over Grasmere at 500ft (150m), or an insensitive farmer is determined to plough up and over an Exmoor hill, there is little that the NPA can do. They desperately need more power and more money. Buying up land that is threatened with development, planting new woodland,

The Forest of Bowland, Lancashire.

(Opposite) Walking on Ben Lomond, Central.

163

building education centres and lobbying MPs and local councillors all consume time and money. And the National Park Authorities, in concert with the people who live and work within the boundaries of the national parks, always keep one eye on the future. Today's decision to build a new visitor centre may lead to tomorrow's noise, litter, pollution and friction with local residents. Today's provision or withdrawal of an EC agricultural subsidy may mean tomorrow's altered landscape. There is also the question of whether more national parks should be designated. The Magnificent Ten, after all, have been in existence since the early 1950s and the countryside has changed radically since then. Only the Norfolk and Suffolk Broads have been added in all that time. What about the Cotswolds, the South Downs, the New Forest, the Lincolnshire Wolds, the central Welsh Borders, or the Lancashire moors?

The NPAs rely for support and advice on their parent body, the Countryside Commission, which in its turn acts as a channel between the NPAs and central government. But it is the large and enthusiastic force of volunteers that really keeps the national parks in good shape – the campaigners and flag-wavers, the ditch-clearers and footpath-markers, the fillers of envelopes and compilers of lists; those who don their anoraks and boots on a bleak February morning to stand their stints as volunteer wardens at some lake or piece of woodland where no one may turn up all day. Individual opinions expressed on such matters as wildlife, footpaths, amenities and development tend to be voices crying in the wilderness. In concert, however, such voices can gain persuasive strength. Many groups and organisations are dedicated to preserving and improving the British countryside, from the friends of tiny local museums to the tens of thousands of members of such powerful bodies as the National Trust and the Ramblers' Association, to whom planners and politicians come for advice and whose objections they ignore at their peril. Without the volunteers and their organisations the countryside would be at far greater risk of exploitation and destruction than it is, and the national parks would probably cease to exist.

THE NEED FOR CONSERVATION

We tend to think of our own age as the only period in history in which wildlife and the landscape have suffered at the hands of man. But we have already seen in Chapter 1 how man's activities began to change the appearance and natural balance of the countryside as soon as he had developed the tools for the job – as far back as the Middle Stone Age, perhaps eight thousand years ago. It could be that some Mesolithic grandpa was grumbling even then about those new-fangled stone cutting tools and the 'disgraceful' destruction of woodland that he had hunted through as a boy! The advent of metal tools, the Romans and their drainage schemes, the Anglo-Saxon clearances, the Norman settlement of towns, medieval sheep runs on the downs, eighteenth-century enclosure and nineteenth-century expansion of towns and industrial devastation – it has been a continuing story. Wildlife suffered far more from the activities of sportsmen in Victorian times than it does today. Consider, for example, Lord Walsingham's bag for one day's shooting on 31 January 1899: 39 pheasants, 6 partridges, 23 mallard, 6 gadwall, 4 pochard, 7 teal, 1 goldeneye, 3 swans, 1 woodcock, 1 snipe, 2 jack snipe, 1 pigeon, 2 herons, 65 coots, 2 moorhens, 9 hares, 16 rabbits, an otter, a rat – and a pike, which he shot as it lay in the shallows! The man simply blasted everything that moved anywhere near him. His dog and beater are reported to have survived the day.

There were the egg-collectors, too, who were proud of their thousands of specimens ; the shooters and stuffers of songbirds for the glass cases of suburbia; the amateur botanists who always collected and took home with them the rarities they found; the butterfly hunters who pinned their prey to display boards; the naturalists who, before the days of photography, could only study birds and beasts that had been shot or trapped. Much of this slaughter, ironically, was inspired by the scientist-writers such as Gilbert White, Charles Darwin and Philip Gosse, who created in their reading public a tremendous thirst for knowledge about the natural world. Man's eternal need to have, hold and possess the things that attracted him played its part, too.

CONSERVATION BODIES

The idea of conservation is not particularly new. Before Queen Victoria came to the throne in 1837 there were already two national botanical societies in Britain. Zoos and botanical gardens were well established during the nineteenth century, as were the Society for the Protection of Birds, the Commons Preservation Society and the National Trust for Places of Historic Interest and Natural Beauty (the National Trust, as it is nowadays rather more widely known). These were followed during this century by the Councils for the Preservation of Rural England (1926), Scotland (1926) and Wales (1928), and the Ulster Society for the Preservation of the Countryside (1937), the Norfolk Naturalists' Trust (1926), the Youth Hostels Association (1935), the Nature Conservancy (1949), the National Parks Commission (1949) and the British Trust for Conservation Volunteers (1959). All these bodies – and many more – have their varying degrees of influence on the countryside. Their capacity to protect, improve and preserve is directly related to the support they receive from ordinary people. It is worth looking a little more closely at the aims and achievements of a few of the main conservation bodies, to appreciate fully their far-reaching influence.

The Countryside Commission was formed in 1968 out of the National Parks Commission that had been set up in 1949 to implement that year's National Parks and Access to the Countryside Act. The Countryside Commission has all the responsibilities borne by the old NPC for the national parks, and in addition advises the government of the day on all matters relating to the conservation of

Tenby Museum, Castle Hill, Tenby, Dyfed, Wales. Among other exhibits of natural and local history, a large late-Victorian egg collection.

Gilbert White Museum, The Wakes, Selborne, Alton, Hampshire. In The Wakes, Gilbert White's old home, now a museum, the original manuscript of his very influential book *The Natural History of Selborne* (1788) may be seen, as well as a display of his life and work as a pioneer ecologist. Garden contains the ha-ha he made, and his melon wall and sundial – many other features added later – and has a view to Selborne Hanger, the beech wood where White built his Zig-Zag path and carried out much of his research.

landscape and leisure use of the countryside – two aims that are often in conflict with each other. The commission has the power to designate a selected area of the country as an Area of Outstanding Natural Beauty (AONB) and any suitable section of coastline as a Heritage Coast. These designations do give a certain amount of protection from destructive or insensitive development, but can be overruled by secretaries of state – particularly in the case of major developments such as road-building. Some examples of the Countryside Commission's work include making grants for tree-planting, recreation schemes and provision of rangers in national parks; forcing through amendments to acts of parliament to protect beautiful countryside owned by national water authorities; publishing leaflets, newspapers and books explaining the commission's work and advising on countryside matters; backing the production of videos to encourage conservation activities at parish and local community level; giving grants and advice to local authorities for planting woodland around cities; lobbying the government to introduce laws to protect fast-vanishing common land from disappearing entirely under concrete or crops.

As we have seen, the hard work and enthusiasm of the voluntary bodies and their members are essential to the well-being and continued survival of the national parks. More than forty of these organisations have banded together under the overall title of the Council for National Parks; they include the Ramblers' Association, the Councils for the Protection of Rural England and Wales, the Youth Hostels Association and the National Trust. They have a wide variety of interests and spheres of activity, but share the common aim of promoting awareness of and interest in the national parks, and fighting off such unwelcome threats as proposals to open new quarries and planning applications for the creation of holiday villages and their attendant roads and services.

Britain's first official conservation body was the Nature Conservancy, which was formed in 1949 at the same time as the National Parks Commission and subsequently became known as the Nature Conservancy Council. Recent governmental policy has seen the conservation duties of the NCC divided between three smaller regional organisations: English Nature, the Nature Conservancy Council for Scotland, and the Countryside Council for Wales. The old NCC played a vital role as an advisory voice, free of all party bias, in the ear of government ministers. There are fears that the separating of its component national parts will seriously weaken Britain's leading position in world conservation, and will prove domestically to be a case of 'divide and overrule'. It would indeed be a very sad development if Britain's nature conservation bodies lost their advisory clout, for the work of the NCC in establishing National Nature Reserves (NNRs) and in designating Sites of Special Scientific Interest (SSSIs) has been one of the strongest strands of nature conservation in this country.

There are nearly 250 National Nature Reserves in Britain, cover-

ing every kind of habitat from salt-marsh to mountain, a huge area of almost 400,000 acres (160,000ha). And these are not just places left to run wild, devoid of human influence. NCC workers and volunteers on the Hebridean island of Rhum, for example, are kept hard at work restoring woodland to sheltered glens, managing the grazing of coastal heath and grassland by Highland cattle, fencing against red deer intrusion, studying and reporting on the lifestyle of those red deer, mending roads and buildings, supervising visitors, collecting all the island's supplies and passengers from the mainland ferry in their own boat, establishing and maintaining nature trails and monitoring the progress of all plant, bird and animal species. Visitors are usually allowed on to NNRs, if they are prepared to go quietly and take advice – although it would be stretching a point to say that all NCC wardens are ecstatic about mixing the reserves with the general public.

Sites of Special Scientific Interest are notified to the relevant local planning authority and their status is confirmed by the appropriate national conservancy council, after which they may or may not be managed as nature reserves. What SSSIs contain are vulnerable wildlife species that are typical of the area, or are worth special care and attention for some other reason. They are often tiny areas which can be wholly destroyed by a housing development or change in agricultural use. In theory, local authorities and owners and occupiers of SSSIs are obliged to consult the Nature Conservancy Council before undertaking any activity that is likely to change or damage their special features. In practice, a quick pre-emptive squirt with a spray or scoop with a digger can circumvent the need for consultation. And, as the national conservancy councils often point out, National Nature Reserves and Sites of Special Scientific Interest, along with the newly designated Marine Nature Reserves in Britain's territorial waters, are not by themselves going to ensure the survival of British wildlife in all its subtle diversity. Everyone, everywhere, has to be educated and become involved. The national conservancy councils help that process along with their many well-illustrated booklets on such topics as acid rain, climate change, planting of broadleaved trees and nature conservation in the countryside and in cities.

The Council for the Protection of Rural England (CPRE) and its counterparts Campaign for the Protection of Rural Wales (CPRW), Association for the Protection of Rural Scotland (APRS) and Ulster Society for the Preservation of the Countryside (USPC) have proved to be among the most effective pressure groups in safeguarding the countryside from bad planning and selfish decision-making. Until the formation of the National Parks Commission and its successor the Countryside Commission, these were just about the only bodies with influence in such matters as maintaining green belts between towns, preventing ribbon development of housing, keeping a restraining hand on quarrying and mining, and restricting damaging planning applications. They are still in the front rank

St Andrews Sealife Centre, The Scores, St Andrews, Fife, Scotland. Hundreds of sea creatures on display in exhibition designed to show them in their natural environment.

of the countryside's watchdogs, keeping the Department of the Environment on its toes and making sure that up-to-the-minute issues are made the subject of public debate and ministerial action – for example, access roads for the Channel Tunnel, new towns proposed by developers, open-cast mining, hedges and their accelerating disappearance from the British landscape, provision of low-cost housing for rural workers, conversion of old barns to new dwellings. The county branches of CPRE, CPRW, APRS and USPC maintain the same vigilance at local level. CPRE's quarterly magazine *Countryside Campaigner* continues the combative approach, ready either to applaud good governmental decisions or to raise the dust over bad ones.

One of the best-known conservation and preservation bodies is the National Trust, which was founded in 1895 to own or to act as guardian of property (buildings, ancient monuments or land) in the national interest. In 1907 the National Trust's properties were declared inalienable in law – that is, they could not be sold or bought without the express permission of parliament. This safeguard has given thousands of property owners a guarantee that passing on or handing over their houses or land to the National Trust will benefit future generations as well as keep their property intact. The Trust looks after most of the Lake District, as well as many miles of coastline, moorland and dales, fenland and downs, forests and pastures, gardens and villages, ancient monuments and historic houses. The National Trusts for Scotland, Wales and Northern Ireland carry on the same work in those countries. Many of the donors or their descendants continue to live in the houses they have given to the National Trust, which usually makes a charge (to non-members) for entry to such properties. But in the hundreds of thousands of countryside acres that belong to the NT, everyone is free to wander where they wish – with due consideration, of course, for farmers and other workers and those living in the area.

Norfolk naturalists were the first in the country to form their own society, the Norfolk Naturalists' Trust, which came into being in 1926. There are over forty of these County Naturalists' Trusts nowadays, each dedicated to conserving, recording and protecting the wildlife on its own patch. They are empowered by central government to establish and maintain nature reserves, and most have done so – these range from half-mile stretches of disused railway line to hundreds of acres of moorland, with every conceivable kind of habitat in between. These trusts are always on the lookout for new members, especially those who are keen to join in with their events and to help with volunteer duties, which can be anything from wardening to manning a stall at a village fête. They usually mix a good deal of fun with their activities – for example, fungal forays at dawn, or bird-watching expeditions that end up in the pub – while for real expertise on all aspects of local natural history you need look no further than their dedicated members, some of half a century's standing or more. The Royal Society for Nature Conserva-

Great Westhay Moor, Somerset, an NCC grant-aided purchase.

(Opposite above) Northumberland – enjoying part of an adventure holiday.

(Opposite below) Gordale Scar near Malham, North Yorkshire.

tion, which is based at Nettleham in Lincolnshire, the RSNC (Wales) in Brecon, the Scottish Wildlife Trust in Edinburgh and the Ulster Wildlife Trust in Belfast act as focal points for the county and local naturalists' trusts, and will supply names, addresses and other details.

In spite of the growing public awareness of the havoc caused by egg-collecting, pollution, indiscriminate shooting and destruction of habitat, the birds of the countryside still face these and other threats to their well-being and, ultimately, their survival. The Society for the Protection of Birds, which was established in Victorian times, added the word 'royal' to its title and became the RSPB in 1904. Since then it has gone from strength to strength, buying up suitable land to create reserves, reinstating threatened areas such as wetland and woodland, opposing development of nesting and breeding sites, advising landowners on ways to safeguard their bird populations and educating and entertaining youngsters through its Young Ornithologists' Club. Regional members' groups carry on the

good work at local level, their ever-swelling membership reflecting the growth of bird-watching into one of the most popular leisure activities for town and country dwellers alike.

The Commons Preservation Society was also established early on in the development of the conservation movement, beginning its defence of commons and other open spaces as far back as 1865. Its members went on to lay the foundations of the National Trust on the long road to becoming today's Open Spaces Society. The society has saved many irreplaceable commons from destruction, enclosure or development, among them such well-known examples as the wide ranges of Epping Forest, Hampstead Heath and Wimbledon Common. There are an estimated 1.5 million acres (600,000ha) of common land in Britain, but public right of access to only one-fifth of that countryside. The slogan of the Open Spaces Society is a simple one – 'Open up the Countryside' – and to that end they lobby for protective laws, for the public's right of access to common land and for footpaths, unobstructed and properly marked, to guarantee that access.

The footpath organisation with the highest public profile is undoubtedly the Ramblers' Association. The catalyst for its creation, by the amalgamation in 1935 of more than three hundred local rambling clubs, was the publicity given to public demand for access to open country by the mass trespasses of the Manchester Ramblers in 1932, when huge crowds of walkers deliberately defied landowners, gamekeepers and the police to flood in their thousands up on to the forbidden moors of the Pennines. The local groups still operate, more than three hundred of them forming the power base of the Ramblers' Association, but the organisation has gained enormous influence at national level as well. With well on the way to a hundred thousand members, the Ramblers – and the famed and feared stinging articles in their quarterly magazine *The Rambler* – simply cannot be ignored when legislation on access to the countryside is under discussion.

It was sustained action by the RA, along with other organisations, that saw Britain's superb network of long-distance footpaths established – action in the lobbies of parliament and action at the grass roots in negotiations with individual landowners, in waymarking, signposting, siting stiles and clearing obstructions. The Pennine Way – 250 miles (400km) of remote moorland walking from Derbyshire to Scotland – is the jewel in the RA crown, but there are many others – the Offa's Dyke path along the Welsh Borders, the South-West Peninsula Coast Path, the South and North Downs Ways, the Ridgeway path from the Chilterns to Wessex, the Peddars Way through East Anglia and the Cleveland Way that curls around the edges of the North York Moors. The RA chivvies local authorities over every aspect of access to particular parts of Britain and makes sure that footpaths are properly mapped and displayed to the public. The activity that gains them most publicity is their contesting of the blockage of footpaths by barbed wire, by ploughing or building over the path, by letting bulls run free, by neglect or ignorance. But they are also hard at work arguing the case against hedge-ripping, road-building, quarrying of unbroken country and the sale of water company and Forestry Commission land.

One way of getting around the countryside without having to spend a fortune on accommodation is to use the far-flung network of youth hostels – there are over 340 of them, scattered all through England, Scotland, Wales and Northern Ireland, ranging from superb old country houses to castles, converted warehouses to simple wooden huts. When the Youth Hostels Association of Great Britain started in 1930 it was very much a rough-and-ready affair. Members simply sought out any suitable building, rolled up their sleeves and converted it themselves. Everything was extremely basic – a place to sleep, a place to cook and some fresh water somewhere nearby was the full tally of requirements of those pre-war hikers with their spartan British 'if-it-hurts-it-must-be-good-for-me' philosophy. Some of those early members regret the recent changes that the YHA has undergone, but for most ramblers and hikers it is a blessed relief to know that the sexes need no longer be segregated, that there will probably be hot showers, lights, heating, perhaps a hot meal provided by the hostel's own cooks, and maybe even a glass of beer in front of the television.

All the organisations detailed so far in this chapter are working in their own ways on the conservation of the environment and many of their members belong to the British Trust for Conservation Volunteers, which was formed in 1959. The BTCV deliberately concentrates on practical projects such as tree-planting, drystone walling, signposting footpaths and laying down boardwalks, clearing rubbish from wetland sites and creating new areas of wetland, converting derelict land in cities into nature reserves, planting and fencing sand-dunes to stop erosion. The Trust is active in schools and in adult training, and produces booklets of practical advice on how to go about a wide range of conservation activities.

In many ways the BTCV is the natural, practical meeting ground of the ideas, dreams and hopes for the future of the British countryside that all the conservation organisations embody. Change is part of the order of things in the countryside – it always has been and it always will be. The pace of change has been accelerating steadily during this century and in some areas seems to be in danger of running out of control. Individuals may feel that there is nothing they can do – it is all being decided and enacted over their heads, whether they like it or not. But the various trusts, societies, associations and councils that are concerned with the countryside offer an excellent opportunity to get involved in a personal, immediate way with the efforts that are being made to halt the decline of wildlife, landscape and rural life. There are 50 million acres (20 million ha) in Britain, most of them rural, every one of them potentially rich and beautiful. Green or black, whole or ruined? We are the ones who decide. It is quite a challenge.

Rock-climbing at Allenhead,
Northumberland.

Menston, Yorkshire.

GAZETTEER

ENGLAND

AVON

* Craft Study Centre
Holburne of Menstrie Museum
Great Pulteney Street
Bath
Tel: 0225-66669
Craft archive, collections, exhibitions

* Woodspring Museum
Burlington Street
Weston-super-Mare
Tel: 0934-21028
Archaeology of area

BUCKINGHAMSHIRE

* Chiltern Open Air Museum
Newland Park
Chalfont St Giles
Tel: 02407-71117
Buildings through the ages; Iron Age and
medieval re-creation experiments

CAMBRIDGESHIRE

* Cambridge & County Folk Museum
2–3 Castle Street
Cambridge
Tel: 0223-355159
Fenland life and tools

* Sacrewell Farm & Country Centre
Thornhaugh
Peterborough
Tel: 0780-782222
Working farm; conservation, bygone tools,
trails

* University Museum of Archaeology and Anthropology
Downing Street
Cambridge
Tel: 0223-333511
Archaeology; anthropology

* Wicken Fen Nature Reserve
Wickhen
Near Soham
Tel: 0353-720274
Undrained fen, full of wildlife; information
centre

CHESHIRE

* National Waterways Museum
Dockyard Road
Ellesmere Port
Tel: 051-355-5017
Narrowboats; inland waterways exhibition

CORNWALL

Padstow Museum
Padstow Institute
Market Street
Padstow
Tel (Padstow Library): 0841-532387
Jumble of local history

* Wayside Museum
Zennor
Tel: 0736-796945
Cornish tin mining, farming, local history

CUMBRIA

Carlisle Museum
Tullie House
Castle Street
Carlisle
Tel: 0228-34781
Romans, local history, wildlife

* Dove Cottage
Town End
Grasmere
Tel: 0966-5544
Wordsworth's house; adjacent museum

* Kendal Museum
Station Road
Kendal
Tel: 0539-721374
Local history, 'nature trail'

* = *featured in text boxes*

* Museum of Lakeland Life and Industry
Abbot Hall
Kendal
Tel: 0539-722464
Local life, farming, industry

* Stott Park Bobbin Mill
Finsthwaite
Lake Windermere
Tel: 0448-31087
Craftsmen making wooden bobbins, etc

Whitehaven Museum
Civic Hall
Lowther Street
Whitehaven
Tel: 0946-67575
Local history, mining, fishing

DERBYSHIRE
* City of Derby Museum
The Strand
Derby
Tel: 0332-255579
Local history; ecology and conservation

DEVON
* Lyn & Exmoor Museum
St Vincent Cottage
Lynton
Tel (Tourist Information Office):
0598-52225
Wonderful mish-mash of Exmoor life and
history

Morwellham Quay
Near Tavistock
Tel: 0822-832766
Copper mine tour, craft workers in
Victorian dress, exhibitions

DORSET
* Dorset County Museum
High West Street
Dorchester
Tel: 0305-62735
Local history, archaeology, Thomas Hardy

* Lyme Regis Museum
Bridge Street,
Lyme Regis
Tel: 0297-43370
Local history, geology

Tithe Barn Museum
Church Hill
Swanage
Tel: 0929-4768
Local history, quarrying

DURHAM
*** Beamish North of England Open Air
Museum**
Beamish Hall
Stanley
Tel: 0207-31811
Drift mine, pit cottages, Victorian market
town, farm, transport and more

EAST SUSSEX
* Clergy House
Alfriston
Tel: 0323-870001
Fourteenth-century priests' house

Lewes Museum
Lewes
Tel: 0273-474379
Lewes Castle; Barbican House, with
Museum of Sussex Archaeology and scale
model of Victorian Lewes; fifteenth-century
timber-framed Anne of Cleves' House
museum

* Sussex Farm Museum Trust
Horam Manor Farm
Heathfield
Tel: 0435-32597
Farming history; nature trails

ESSEX
Hythe Quay Maritime Centre
Hythe Quay
Maldon
Tel: 0621-856503
Local history; coastal barges

* John Webb's Windmill
Thaxted
Tel: 0371-830366
Windmill under restoration; local history
museum

*** Maldon District Agriculture and
Domestic Museum**
47 Church Street
Goldhanger
Maldon
Tel: 0621-88647/53856
Tractors, farm and domestic implements

GAZETTEER

Southchurch Hall
Southend-on-Sea
Tel: 0702-467671
Fourteenth-century hall

GLOUCESTERSHIRE

Gloucester Folk Museum
99–103 Westgate Street
Gloucester
Tel: 0452-26467
Local history; many displays

* **National Waterways Museum**
Gloucester Docks
Gloucester
Tel: 0452-307009
Narrowboats, story of inland waterways

* **Ruskin Mill**
Nailsworth
Tel: 0453-62571
Craft workshops in restored textile mill

* **Westonbirt Arboretum**
Near Tetbury
Tel: 0666-88220
Great variety of trees

Wildfowl Trust
Slimbridge
Tel: 0453-89333
Waterfowl from all over the world

HAMPSHIRE

* **Gilbert White Museum**
The Wakes
Selborne
Alton
Tel: 0420-50303
House, garden and writings of pioneer ecologist

* **Manor Farm**
Upper Hamble Country Park
Botley
Near Southampton
Tel: 0489-787055
Working Victorian farm; animals, implements, workshops, events, walks

Selborne Circle of Rural Writers
Selborne Cottage Shop
Selborne
Alton
Tel: 0420-50307
Information, meetings, interest in countryside writers

* **Stubbs Farm**
Kingsley
Bordon
Tel: 0420-34906
Walks round family farm

HEREFORD & WORCESTER

* **Avoncroft Museum of Buildings**
Stoke Heath
Bromsgrove
Worcestershire
Tel: 0527-31363
Buildings through the ages, saved from demolition

* **Dunkerton's Cider Company**
Hays Head
Luntley
Pembridge
Leominster
Herefordshire
Tel: 0544-7653
Varieties of cider and perry, rare apple trees planted

* **Elgar's Birthplace**
Crown East Lane
Lower Broadheath
Worcester
Worcestershire
Tel: 0905-66224
Composer's scores, personal items

* **Hergest Croft Gardens**
Kington
Herefordshire
Tel: 0544-230160
Mature gardens, trees, rhododendrons

* **Old Grammar School Heritage Centre**
Church Lane
Ledbury
Herefordshire
Tel: 0531-5680
Local and architectural history in Tudor building

Old House Museum
High Town
Hereford
Herefordshire
Tel: 0432-268121 ext 225
Jacobean house and furnishings

177

HERTFORDSHIRE
* Mill Green Water Mill
Mill Green
Hatfield
Tel: 0707-271362
Working water-mill, local history museum, events

KENT
* Cobtree Museum of Kent Rural Life
Lock Lane
Cobtree Manor Park
Sandling
Maidstone
Tel: 0622-763936
Traditional farm practices; demonstrations

LEICESTERSHIRE
Rutland County Museum
Catmose Street
Oakham
Rutland
Tel: 0572-723654
Rural life in Rutland through the ages

LINCOLNSHIRE
Church Farm Museum
Church Road South
Skegness
Tel: 0754-66658
Lincolnshire farming

* Gibraltar Point Nature Reserve
Near Skegness
Tel: 0754-2677
Visitor centre, displays; shore, sand and marsh walks

Millstone Craft Centre
Hogsthorpe
Near Skegness
Tel: 0754-72977
Pottery, bronze, rosewood working

MERSEYSIDE
* Wirral Country Park Visitor Centre
Station Road
Thurstaston
Wirral
Tel: 051-648-4371
Displays on geology, wildlife, creation of 12-mile (19-km) linear park on disused railway line

NORFOLK
Black Sheep
Ingworth
Norwich
Tel: 0263-733142/732006
Wool, knitwear

* Broadland Conservation Centre
Ranworth Broad
Near Norwich
Tel: 0605-49479
Nature trail; floating exhibition centre

Broadland Information Centre
Station Road
Hoveton
Tel: 0605-32281
Ecology and conservation

* Broads Museum
Sutton Windmill
Near Stalham
Tel: 0692-81195
Restored windmill; natural history and conservation of Norfolk Broads

Cromer Museum
East Cottages
Tucker Street
Cromer
Tel: 0263-513543
Local history, fishing, tourism

English Lavender
Caley Mill
Heacham
Tel: 0485-70384
Lavender and rose gardens, shop, guided tour

* Norfolk Shire Horse Centre
West Runton Stables
West Runton
Cromer
Tel: 0263-75339
Working shire horses

NORTH HUMBERSIDE
Flamborough Head Heritage Information Centre
South Landing
Flamborough
Tel: 0262-850819
Wildlife, village traditions, guided walks

NORTHUMBERLAND
* Clayton Memorial Museum
Chesters Roman Fort
Walwick
Near Hexham
Tel: 0434-681379
Wide range of Roman remains

NORTH YORKSHIRE
* ARC Archaeological Resource Centre
St Saviourgate
York
Tel: 0904-643211
Hands-on archaeology

* Brimham Rocks Information Centre
Brimham House
Summerbridge
Harrogate
Tel: 0423-780688
Exhibition on millstone grit landscape

* Jorvik Viking Centre
Coppergate
York
Tel: 0904-643211
'Time travel' through reconstructed Viking
settlement

* Merchant Adventurers' Hall
Fossgate
York
Tel: 0904-654818
Fourteenth-century timber-framed
Guildhall

Robin Hood's Bay Museum
Fishergate
Robin Hood's Bay
Tel: 0947-880241
Local history, fishing

* Ryedale Folk Museum
Hutton-le-Hole
York
Tel: 0751-5367
Buildings, country crafts and livelihoods

Woodend Museum
The Crescent
Scarborough
Tel: 0723-367326
Local natural history and geology,
conservatory, aquarium; in former home of
Sitwell family – Sitwell exhibition

* Yorkshire Museum
Museum Gardens
York
Tel: 0904-629745
Life from Roman to medieval times

SOMERSET
Barrington Court
Barrington
Ilminster
Tel: 0460-40601/52242
Tudor house, gardens, kitchen garden,
estate trail, farm exhibition centre, events

* New Road Farm
East Huntspill
Somerset
Tel: 0278-783250
Working farm; children's activities, nature
trails, visitor centre

* P. A. Coate & Son
Meare Green Court
Stoke St Gregory
Taunton
Tel: 0823-490249
Willow weaving through all its processes

Perry's Cider Mills
Dowlish Wake
Tel: 0460-52681
Traditional cider

* Quantock Weavers
The Old Forge
Plainsfield
Over Stowey
Bridgwater
Tel: 0278-67687
Hand-spun, hand-knitted and woven,
naturally dyed products

* Somerset Rural Life Museum
Abbey Farm
Chilkwell Street
Glastonbury
Tel: 0458-31197
Fourteenth-century barn, Victorian farm life
and work display, theme trails, events

* Willows Peat Moors Visitor Centre
Shapwick Road
Westhay
Glastonbury
Tel: 0458-6257
Peat-cutting history and demonstrations;
reconstruction of ancient marsh trackway;
wildlife of Somerset Levels

SOUTH YORKSHIRE
* Sheffield City Museum
Weston Park
Sheffield
Tel: 0742-768588
Development of Sheffield and its industries

SUFFOLK
* Bridge Cottage
Flatford
East Bergholt
Tel: 0206-298260
Exhibition of John Constable's landscape
and painting

Dunwich Museum
Dunwich
Tel: 0728-73358
Relief model and display on erosion and
destruction of medieval Dunwich by the sea

Kentwell Hall
Long Melford
Tel: 0787-310207
Tudor mansion, gardens, rare breeds;
Tudor life enacted

* Kersey Pottery
The Street
Kersey
Tel: 0473-822092
Pottery can be seen being made

* Lavenham Guildhall
Lavenham
Tel: 0787-248207
Tudor Guildhall; exhibition of medieval
wool trade

* Museum of East Anglian Life
Stowmarket
Tel: 0449-612229
Buildings, collections, displays of East
Anglian work and life

* Otter Trust
Earsham
Bungay
Tel: 0986-893470
World's largest collection of otters

* Thetford Forest Information Centre
Santon Downham
Near Brandon
Tel: 0842-810271
Woodland display, information, walks

SURREY
Old Kiln Museum
Reeds Road
Tilford
Farnham
Tel: 0251-252300
Wheelwright's shop, farm carts and tools,
forestry display, events

WEST SUSSEX
* Amberley Chalk Pits Museum
Amberley
Near Arundel
Tel: 0798-81370
Lime kilns, workshops, industrial displays

*** Weald and Downland Open Air
Museum**
Singleton
Near Chichester
Tel: 0243-63348
Buildings through the ages; walks

Wildfowl Trust
Arundel
Tel: 0903-883355
Wildfowl from all over the world

WEST YORKSHIRE
* Shibden Hall Folk Museum
Godley Lane
Halifax
Tel: 0422-352246
Agricultural and craft work and life in the
Pennines

* Yorkshire Mining Museum
Caphouse Colliery
New Road
Overton
Wakefield
Tel: 0924-848806
Tour of coal mine, mining exhibition, nature
trail

WILTSHIRE

* Alexander Keiller Museum
Avebury
Tel: 0672-3250
Archaeological exhibition, display of local finds

Great Barn Museum of Wiltshire Folk Life
Avebury
Tel: 0672-3555
Agricultural life and work through the ages in Wiltshire

* Salisbury & South Wiltshire Museum
The King's House
65 The Close
Salisbury
Tel: 0722-332151
Displays and collections – early man to medieval

* Stourhead House
Stourton
Near Mere
Tel: 0747-840348
Eighteenth-century mansion and landscaped grounds; trees, walks

WALES

CLWYD

* Chwarel Wynne Slate Mine and Museum
Glyn Ceiriog
Near Llangollen
Tel: 0691-72343
Guided tour of slate mine; display of life in Victorian slate-mining village

* Geological Museum of North Wales
Bwlchgwyn
Near Wrexham
Tel: 0978-757573
Geological displays, specimen garden, quarry trail

DYFED

Carmarthen Museum
Abergwili
Carmarthen
Tel: 0267-231691
Local history and agriculture

Penrhos Traditional Welsh Cottage
Penrhos
Llanycefn
Haverfordwest
Tel: 0267-233333
Restored to original condition

* Rhos-ddu Farm
Crymych
Cardigan
Tel: 0239-73220
Working farm with trails; supervised join-in activities for children

Scolton Manor Heritage Park
Scolton
Spittal
Haverfordwest
Tel: 0437-82328
Manor house, country park, arboretum

* Tenby Museum
Castle Hill
Tenby
Tel: 0834-2809
Local history, Victorian egg collection, shells, local wildlife

* Tregwynt Woollen Mill
Near St Nicholas
Letterston
Haverfordwest
Tel: 0348-5225
Working woollen mill; visitors watch, buy and bathe on lovely nearby beaches

GWYNEDD

Penrhyn Castle Industrial Railway Museum
Bangor
Tel: 0248-353084
Locomotives, trucks, track, history

MID-GLAMORGAN

* Ewenny Pottery
Bridgend
Tel: 0656-3020
Long-established family pottery; public welcome to watch

* Heritage Centre
Seamouth
Southerndown
Bridgend
Tel: 0656-880157
Coast and cliff conservation, story of Dunraven Castle

POWYS
* Centre for Alternative Technology
Llwyngwern Quarry
Pantperthog
Machynlleth
Tel: 0654-702400
Every kind of alternative technology,
demonstrated and in practical use

Ceredigion Museum
The Coliseum
Aberystwyth
Tel: 0970-617911
Local history, natural history

* Offa's Dyke Heritage Centre
West Street
Knighton
Tel: 0547-528192/528753
Exhibition on Offa's Dyke and footpath,
riverside park, youth hostel attached

* Robert Owen Memorial Museum
Broad Street
Newtown
Tel: 0686-26345
Life and work of pioneer industrial welfare
champion

SOUTH GLAMORGAN
* Cosmeston Medieval Village
Lavernock Road
Penarth
Tel: 0222-708686
Excavation and finds of Black Death village

Welsh Hawking Centre
Weycock Road
Barry
Tel: 046-734687
Birds of prey from all over the world

WEST GLAMORGAN
* Oxwich National Nature Reserve
Oxwich
Gower
Tel: 0792-390320
Visitor Centre with exhibition, nature trails
through sand-dunes, marsh and woodland

SCOTLAND

BORDERS
* Border Collie and Shepherd Centre
Tweedhopefoot
Tweedsmuir
Tel: 0899-7267
Photographic exhibition of shepherding;
sheepdog handling demonstrations

* Woodland Visitor Centre
Monteviot
Jedburgh
Tel: 0835-3306
Woodlands and timber exhibition; walks

CENTRAL
* Queen Elizabeth Forest Park
Aberfoyle
Tel: 0877-2258
Visitor Centre with exhibition; forest trails

DUMFRIES & GALLOWAY
* Blowplain Open Farm
Balmaclellan
Castle Douglas
Tel: 0644-2206
Farm tours

* Galloway Deer Museum
Clatteringshaws
Near New Galloway
Tel: 0644-2285
Deer collection

* Galloway Farm Museum
New Galloway
Tel: 0644-3317
Farm horses and horse implements at work

FIFE
Cambo
Kingsbarns
Crail
St Andrews
Tel: 0333-50810
Tame farm animals in Cuddle Corner,
adventure play area, nature trail

* Fife Folk Museum
The Weigh House
Ceres
Cupar
Tel: 0334-82250
Fife agriculture, crafts, traditional life

* **Scottish Deer Centre**
Bow of Fife
Cupar
Tel: 0337-81391
Deer tour

Scottish Fisheries Museum
Harbourhead
Anstruther
Tel: 0333-310628
Story of Scottish fishing, brilliantly
displayed

* **St Andrews Sealife Centre**
The Scores
St Andrews
Tel: 0334-72950
Sea creatures in their own environments

GRAMPIAN

Braeloine Interpretive Centre
Glen Tanar
Near Aboyne
Tel: 0339-886072
Wildlife and land use on twentieth-century
estate

Fochabers Folk Museum
Fochabers
Tel: 0343-820362
Collection of horse-drawn carts, local
history

* **Forvie Nature Reserve**
Collieston
Tel: 0368-87330
Visitor Centre with exhibition

North East Falconry Centre
Banff
Tel: 0261-6602
Falcons, hawks, owls; flying displays

* **North-East of Scotland Agricultural
Heritage Centre**
Aden Country Park
Old Deer
Near Peterhead
Tel: 0771-22857
Twentieth-century life on an estate; two
hundred years of farming in Scotland's
north-east

* **Northfield Farm Museum**
New Aberdour
Near Fraserburgh
Tel: 0771-7504
Bygone farm equipment and household
bric-a-brac

St Cyrus Nature Reserve
St Cyrus
Montrose
Tel: 0674-83736
Visitor Centre, botanical and ornithological
displays

HIGHLAND

**Ardnamurchan Natural History and
Visitor Centre**
Glenborrodale
Near Salen
Tel: 0972-4254
Wildlife and ecology

Cairngorm Reindeer Centre
Reindeer House
Loch Morlich
Tel: 0479-86228
Reindeer

Darnaway Farm Visitor Centre
Forres
Tel: 0309-72213
Exhibition of farming and forestry

* **Farigaig Forest Centre**
Inverfarigaig
Loch Ness
Tel: 0463-791575
Conservation; walks

Highland Folk Museum
Kingussie
Tel: 0540-661307
Farming; tinkers

Lhaidhay Caithness Croft Museum
Dunbeath
Tel: 0593-3244
Traditional croft

* **Loch Garten Nature Reserve**
Near Aviemore
Tel: 0479-83694
Osprey viewing; walks

ISLANDS

Colbost Folk Museum
Dunvegan
Isle of Skye
Tel: 0470-22296
Traditional thatched blackhouse

Lewis Black House
Arnol
Isle of Lewis
Outer Hebrides
Tel: 031-244-3101
Traditional blackhouse

Old Byre
Dervaig
Isle of Mull
Tel: 0688-4229
Mull animal and bird life

* Shetland Croft House Museum
Southvoe
Dunrossness
Shetland Mainland
Tel: 0595-5057
Shetland croft house furnished c1860

* Tingwall Agricultural Museum
Veensgarth
Lerwick
Shetland Mainland
Tel: 0595-84344
Shetland crofting and craft tools

LOTHIAN

* Lady Victoria Colliery
Newtongrange
Near Dalkeith
Tel: 031-663-7519
Tour of Victorian colliery; Visitor Centre
display; coal heritage trail

STRATHCLYDE

* Auchindrain Old Highland Township
Inveraray
Tel: 0499-5235
Traditional Highland life through the ages

* Blackshaw Farm Park
Near West Kilbride
Tel: 0563-34257
Working farm

* New Lanark
Tel: 0555-61345
Restored cotton mill settlement

TAYSIDE

Atholl Country Collection
Blair Atholl
Tel: 0796-81232
Display – flax growing and spinning

* Camperdown Wildlife Centre
Dundee
Tel: 0382-623555
Scottish mountain and moorland wildlife

* Meikleour Beech Hedge
Meikleour
Near Perth
Tallest hedge in the world

* Vane Farm Nature Centre
Near Kinross
Loch Leven
Tel: 0577-62355
Displays, bird-watching on loch

* Weaver's House and Highland Tryst Museum
64 Burrell Street
Crieff
Tel: 0764-5202
Tartan weaving; clan archive

NORTHERN IRELAND

ANTRIM

Giant's Causeway Centre
Near Portrush
Tel: (026 57) 31855
Exhibition on natural and social history of
area, and on Giant's Causeway

Lagan Valley Regional Park
Tel: (0232) 491922
10-mile (16-km) towpath walk along River
Lagan

Leslie Hill Historic Farm and Park
Martin Road
Ballymoney
Tel: (026 56) 63109
Carriage display in eighteenth-century
outbuildings, pets' corner, family museum

Loughside Open Dairy Farm
17 Island Road Lower
Ballycarry
Tel: (096 03) 53312
Friesian Holstein herd, highland cattle, red
deer, vixens at pets' corner

Portrush Countryside Centre
Bath Road
Portrush
Tel: (0265) 823600
Geology; fossils; conservation

Shane's Castle Railway
Randalstown Road
Antrim
Tel: (084 94) 28216
Nature reserve has birdwatching hides,
narrow-gauge steam railway

Streamvale Open Dairy Farm
38 Ballyhanwood Road
Belfast
Tel: (0232) 483244
Milking, pets' corner, nature trail

Watertop Open Farm
188 Cushendall Road
Ballycastle
Tel: (026 87) 62676/63785
Ornamental game birds, paddiwagon tours,
sheep shearing demonstrations, pony
trekking, lakeside barbecues

ARMAGH
**Oxford Island National Nature
Reserve**
Signposted at Exit 10 M1
Tel: (0762) 322205
Wildlife exhibition at Visitor Centre, bird-
watching hides, walks, picnic areas

Peatlands Country Park
Craigavon
Tel: (0762) 851102
Visitor Centre and outdoor exhibits on peat
ecology; narrow-gauge railway trips to peat
bog

DOWN
Ark Open Farm
296 Bangor Road
Newtownards
Tel: (0247) 812672/820445
Rare breeds, pony rides, pets' corner

Crawfordsburn Country Park
Tel: (0247) 853621
Visitor Centre; coastal, riverside and
woodland walks

Mourne Countryside Centre
91 Central Promenade
Newcastle
Tel: (039 67) 24059
Complete information on Mourne
Mountains

Scrabo Country Park
Newtownards
Tel: (0247) 811491
Scrabo Tower Countryside Centre;
woodland walks; geology

Ulster Folk & Transport Museum
Cultra
Near Holywood
Tel: (0232) 428428
Open-air folk museum with original
farmhouses, watermills, small village,
church and shops rebuilt on site. Transport
section includes donkey creels and other
rural transport

Wildfowl & Wetlands Trust
Castle Espie
78 Ballydrain Road
Comber
Resident mute swans among wildfowl
collection

FERMANAGH
Castle Archdale Country Park
Kesh
Tel: (036 56) 21588
Natural history exhibition, archaeology,
marina, lakeshore walks

LONDONDERRY
Roe Valley Country Park
Dog Leap
Limavady
Tel: (050 47) 22074
Local history museum; visitor centre;
fishing, canoeing, rock climbing.

The Ness Country Park
Claudy
Tel: (050 47) 22074
Woodland nature trails; Northern Ireland's
highest waterfall

TYRONE

Lisahoppin Open Farm
2 Leap Lane
Omagh
Tel: (0662) 242502
Dairy farm at work, milking, nature trail,
riverside walk

Sperrin Heritage Centre
274 Glenelly Road
Gortin
Tel: (066 26) 48142
Natural history, panning for gold in iron
pyrites stream

Ulster History Park
Cullion
Omagh
Tel: (066 26) 48188
Houses and monuments of Ireland from
9,000 years ago to seventeenth century

ADDRESSES

THE COUNTRYSIDE COMMISSION
John Dower House
Crescent Place
Cheltenham
Gloucestershire GL50 3RA
Tel: 0242-521381

COUNTRYSIDE COMMISSION FOR SCOTLAND
Battleby
Redgorton
Perth PH1 3EW
Scotland
Tel: 0738-27921

COUNTRYSIDE COUNCIL FOR WALES
Plas Penrhos
Ffordd Penrhos
Bangor
Gwynedd LL57 2LQ
Wales
Tel: 0248-370444

COUNCIL FOR NATIONAL PARKS
45 Shelton Street
London WC2H 9HJ
Tel: 071-924-4077

SCOTTISH COUNCIL FOR NATIONAL PARKS
15 Park Terrace
Stirling FK8 2JT
Central Region
Scotland
Tel: 0786-65714

ENGLISH NATURE
Northminster House
Peterborough
Cambridgeshire PE1 1UA
Tel: 0733-340345

NATURE CONSERVANCY COUNCIL FOR SCOTLAND
12 Hope Terrace
Edinburgh EH9 2AS
Scotland
Tel: 031-447-4784

COUNTRYSIDE COUNCIL FOR WALES
(see 'Countryside Commission')

Northern Ireland: contact
INTERNATIONAL BRANCH OF ENGLISH NATURE
Northminster House
Peterborough
Cambridgeshire PE1 1UA
Tel: 0733-62626

COUNCIL FOR THE PROTECTION OF RURAL ENGLAND
Warwick House
25 Buckingham Palace Road
London SW1W 0PP
Tel: 071-976-6433

ASSOCIATION FOR THE PROTECTION OF RURAL SCOTLAND
14A Napier Road
Edinburgh EH10 5AY
Scotland
Tel: 031-229-1898

CAMPAIGN FOR THE PROTECTION OF RURAL WALES
Ty Gwyn
31 High Street
Welshpool
Powys SY21 7JP
Wales
Tel: 0938-552525

ULSTER SOCIETY FOR THE PRESERVATION OF THE COUNTRYSIDE
Peskett House
2/2A Windsor Road
Belfast 9
Northern Ireland
Tel: 0232-381304

NATIONAL TRUST
36 Queen Anne's Gate
London SW1H 9AS
Tel: 071-222-9251

NATIONAL TRUST FOR SCOTLAND
5 Charlotte Square
Edinburgh EH2 4DV
Scotland
Tel: 031-226-5922

NATIONAL TRUST (SOUTH WALES REGION)
The King's Head
Bridge Street
Llandeilo
Dyfed SA19 6BN
Wales
Tel: 0558-822800

NATIONAL TRUST (NORTH WALES REGION)
Trinity Square
Llandudno
Gwynedd LL30 2DE
Wales
Tel: 0492-860123

NATIONAL TRUST (NORTHERN IRELAND)
Rowallane House
Saintfield
County Down BT23 7LH
Northern Ireland
Tel: 0238-510721

ROYAL SOCIETY FOR NATURE CONSERVATION
The Green
Nettleham
Lincoln LN2 2NR
Tel: 0522-544400

SCOTTISH WILDLIFE TRUST
25 Johnston Terrace
Edinburgh EH1 2NH
Scotland
Tel: 031-226-4602

RSNC
THE WILDLIFE TRUSTS PARTNERSHIP (WALES)
c/o Brecknock Wildlife Trust
Lion House
Lion Yard
Brecon
Powys LD3 7AY
Wales
Tel: 0874-5708

ULSTER WILDLIFE TRUST
Barnett's Cottage
Barnett Demesne
Malone Road
Belfast BT9 5PB
Northern Ireland
Tel: 0232-612235

ROYAL SOCIETY FOR THE PROTECTION OF BIRDS
The Lodge
Sandy
Bedfordshire SG19 2BR
Tel: 0767-680551

RSPB (WALES)
Bryn Aderyn
The Bank
Newtown
Powys SY16 2AB
Wales
Tel: 0686-626678

RSPB (NORTHERN IRELAND OFFICE)
Belvoir Park Forest
Belfast BT8 4QT
Northern Ireland
Tel: 0232-491547

RSPB (SCOTLAND)
17 Regent Terrace
Edinburgh EH7 5BN
Scotland
Tel: 031-557-3136

THE OPEN SPACES SOCIETY
25A Bell Street
Henley-on-Thames
Oxfordshire RG9 2BA
Tel: 0491-573535

RAMBLERS' ASSOCIATION
1/5 Wandsworth Road
London SW8 2XX
Tel: 071-582-6878

RAMBLERS' ASSOCIATION (SCOTTISH OFFICE)
Kelinbank
Church Place
Frenchie
Fife KY7 7EP
Scotland
Tel: 0337-58065

RAMBLERS' ASSOCIATION (WALES AREA)
Pantwood
Pant Lane
Marford
Wrexham
Clwyd LL12 8SG
Wales
Tel: 0978-855148

ULSTER FEDERATION OF RAMBLING CLUBS
c/o 27 Slievegallion Drive
Belfast BT11 8JN
Northern Ireland
Tel: 0232-624289

YOUTH HOSTELS ASSOCIATION
Trevelyan House
8 St Stephen's Hill
St Albans
Hertfordshire AL1 2DY
Tel: 0727-45047

SCOTTISH YOUTH HOSTELS ASSOCIATION
7 Glebe Crescent
Stirling
Central Region FK8 2JA
Scotland
Tel: 0786-51181

YOUTH HOSTELS ASSOCIATION (WALES AREA)
4th Floor
1 Cathedral Road
Cardiff
South Glamorgan CF1 9HA
Wales
Tel: 0222-396766

YOUTH HOSTELS ASSOCIATION OF
NORTHERN IRELAND
56 Bradbury Place
Belfast BT7 1RU
Northern Ireland
Tel: 0232-324733

BRITISH TRUST FOR CONSERVATION VOLUNTEERS
36 St Mary's Street
Wallingford
Oxfordshire OX10 0EU
Tel: 0491-39766

CONSERVATION VOLUNTEERS OF
NORTHERN IRELAND
Cherryvale Playing Fields
Ravenhill Road
Belfast BT6 0BZ
Northern Ireland
Tel: 0232-645169

BRITISH TRUST FOR CONSERVATION VOLUNTEERS
(WALES SECTION)
Frolic House
Frolic Street
Newtown
Powys SY16 1AP
Wales
Tel: 0686-628600

SCOTTISH CONSERVATION PROJECT
Balallan House
24 Allan Park
Stirling FK8 2QG
Scotland
Tel: 0786-79697

INDEX